Unemployment, Crime, and Offenders

Unemployment, Crime, and Offenders

Iain Crow
Paul Richardson
Carol Riddington
Frances Simon

Routledge
London and New York

First published 1989
by Routledge
11 New Fetter Lane, London EC4P 4EE
29 West 35th Street, New York, NY 1001

Set in 10/11 pt Times
by Witwell Ltd, Southport

Printed in Great Britain by Billing & Sons Ltd, Worcester

British Library Cataloguing in Publication Data
Unemployment, crime and offenders.
  1. Great Britain. Offenders. Treatment
  I. Crow, Iain
  364.6'0941
  ISBN 0-415-01834-X

Library of Congress Cataloging in Publication Data available

For Margaret, Mick, and John

Man [sic], the more he gains freedom in the sense of emerging from the original oneness with man and nature and the more he becomes an 'individual', has no choice but to unite himself with the world in the spontaneity of love and productive work or else to seek a kind of security by such ties with the world as destroy his freedom and the integrity of his individual self.

Erich Fromm, *Fear of Freedom*

Contents

Contents

Acknowledgements

The original research reported in this book was done with the help of grants from the Economic and Social Research Council (Award no. E00232050), the Leverhulme Trust and the Barrow and Geraldine S. Cadbury Trust. We are most grateful to these bodies for their assistance, without which this book would not have been possible.

Nor could it have been produced without generous donations of time and willing assistance from many people in magistrates' courts, probation and social services and police forces, and the staff of NACRO in various parts of the country. We would also like to thank officials of the Home Office and the Manpower Services Commission for their help. We owe a debt of gratitude to the many defendants and participants in employment and training schemes whose experiences are represented in these pages and hope that a faithful presentation of those experiences goes some way towards repaying that debt.

We have been helped at various times by fellow researchers and colleagues in NACRO who have commented on our work and pointed us towards sources of information. In particular we would like to thank the members of the NACRO Research Committee. Their advice during the period of the two fieldwork projects reported here was invaluable.

Finally, we thank Deloris Carby and Debbie Davenport, secretaries at the NACRO Research Unit at different times, not only for putting in many hours at the typewriter, but for seeing that a number of practical matters were dealt with efficiently.

In recording our thanks to all those who have helped us, however, we would emphasise that what is presented here is, for better or worse, our responsibility alone. Any views and opinions expressed are those of the authors and do not necessarily represent the policy of NACRO or any other individual or body.

Chapter one

The links between unemployment and crime

Asked to list the topics they think have been of greatest public concern in recent years, most people would probably include both unemployment and crime. There has also been a good deal of speculation about the possibility of a link between the two, particularly in the wake of the inner city disturbances that occurred in 1981 and 1985. Much of the debate has been ideological in nature, with the protagonists for and against a link seldom weighing the evidence or considering the complexity of the issues. Furthermore, the preoccupation with the unemployment-crime link has meant that a number of other concerns about the way that unemployment affects the criminal justice system, and ways of dealing with offenders, have been largely ignored.

This book is principally concerned with these other, forgotten issues. It brings together research from a variety of sources undertaken over a number of years, and that undertaken by the NACRO Research Unit, principally between 1984 and 1986. During that time the Unit carried out two studies relating to unemployment. One study, funded by the Economic and Social Research Council, looked at the impact of unemployment on the work of the courts and related agencies, such as the Probation Service. The other study, funded by the Leverhulme Trust, was an evaluation of Youth Training and Community Programme schemes run by NACRO for unemployed people, including a high proportion of offenders. Together these two projects tell us a lot about the practical, day-to-day experiences of dealing with offenders at a time of high unemployment. They also have wider policy implications.

Before the research projects are described in more detail, it is necessary to look at the context in which they are set. There is a wide range of literature relating to unemployment, crime and offenders. No attempt will be made here to present a comprehensive review of this literature, but it is relevant to what follows in later chapters to outline the issues involved.

1

Crime and the economy

Unemployment is but one indicator of the state of an economy. Other measures include gross national product, the retail price index and the level of growth. The distribution of resources and income within an economy is also important. It is therefore necessary to look at the economy as a whole. There can be little doubt that the state of the economy has considerable implications for a country's social, health, educational and other institutions, so it would be surprising if crime and criminal justice were an exception.

As early as 1922 a relationship was reported between criminal conviction rates and the index of business activity in the United States (Ogburn and Thomas 1922). A study of the business cycle for the first half of the twentieth century showed a substantial correlation between low levels of business activity and high levels of property crime (Henry and Short 1954). In the 1960s an American economist undertook a detailed analysis of the relationship between income and delinquency (Fleisher 1969). He noted that economic conditions in general had an effect on delinquency, but that the impact of income levels was particularly marked:

> It appears that the effect of income on delinquency is not a small one. In extremely delinquent areas a one per cent rise in incomes may well cause a 2.5 per cent decline in the rate of delinquency. (Fleisher 1969: 134)

He also presented estimates of the impact of unemployment suggesting that a 50 per cent reduction in unemployment rates in areas where 10 per cent of the labour force is unemployed could reduce the delinquency rate by 10 per cent.

A more recent report by the United Nations Social Defence Research Institute (UNSDRI 1976) underlined the importance of distinguishing between different types of crime. Some crimes, theft of motor vehicles for example, tend to be more characteristic of periods of affluence because of greater opportunities to commit such crimes (e.g. Wilkins 1963). Economic recession, however, was found to be accompanied by a rise in most other forms of property crime and petty 'social' crimes, such as vagrancy and drunkenness. The report also refers to the possibility of what it calls 'sharp crisis scenarios', when looting and street crime occur. In a time-series analysis of crime and economic indicators carried out for data from several countries since the beginning of the century, Harvey Brenner claimed to show strong associations between increased crime and poor economic performance (in UNSDRI 1976).

Such studies appear to provide persuasive evidence that adverse economic conditions are accompanied by a worsening crime problem. This appearance must be qualified to some extent, however. First, the studies may be criticized for using weak or out-dated methods, sometimes with inadequate measures and crude, aggregated data. Second, the crucial words are 'accompanied by': an association between two phenomena does not necessarily mean there is a causal link. For a start it must be shown that the economic decline precedes changes in crime rates and is not merely the accompaniment. Furthermore consideration must be given to whether other factors are involved and to the possible mechanisms that might link one factor to another. If a link exists, then it may be a complex or tenuous one. For example, the UNSDRI report suggests that it may be the very fact of a change in economic conditions that produces greater crime as much as the direction of that change. Another frequently invoked mechanism is the concept of 'relative deprivation': people's expectations and perceptions of how well off they are may be as important as their objective socio-economic situation. A Home Office study of public disorder published in 1982 referred to relative deprivation as a possible source of the riots in US cities in the 1960s (Field and Southgate 1982).

The same study mentioned the complexity of the relationship between disorder and economic circumstances, suggesting that it is not so much individual deprivation as community expectations that are important: 'The inference to be drawn is that the causal route from deprivation to riots is real but complex' (p. 14). This seems to be a reasonable summing up of what we can conclude about the relationship between crime and the economy in general.

Unemployment and crime

Similar considerations apply to the more specific hypothesized relationship between unemployment and crime. The possibility of a link between unemployment and crime is not a recent topic of interest. In 1940 Mannheim examined the plausibility of such a link during the Depression years. He found that 'The movement of crime corresponds fairly accurately to the fluctuations of unemployment' (Mannheim 1940: 43). However, he counselled against relying on global measures of crime and unemployment, suggesting that the relationship could vary depending on other factors. He also noted the potential long-term effects that unemployment could have: 'Long-term unemployment may show its effect even many years after being brought to an end and it is capable of changing permanently the whole attitude of a family towards society' (Mannheim 1940: 41).

Since then a number of studies have considered the possibility of an unemployment-crime link. We have recorded over twenty references which relate specifically to this issue and a Home Office researcher reviewing the literature (Tarling 1982) examined thirty studies. They come to widely varying conclusions. A few writers believe the link is negligible (e.g. Vold 1958). At the other extreme are a small number of studies which conclude that unemployment is a major crime-producing agent. Foremost amongst this latter group has been Harvey Brenner (1976a and b) who has carried out detailed statistical analyses on data from several countries. In between are a larger number of studies and reviewers who believe that unemployment does contribute to the level of crime, but that it is only one of many factors. Opinions vary on how important unemployment is compared to these other factors. Tarling (1982: 32), for example, concluded that 'some evidence of a relationship persists suggesting that unemployment is a factor in the causation of crime, although it may not be a major factor'.

One possible explanation for such a range of conclusions is that more than one study is right: the unemployment-crime relationship is a variable one, manifesting itself under certain conditions but not others. However, a more likely explanation is that different ways of studying the relationship have been used and that the conclusions depend on the methods employed. Broadly speaking two main types of study have been used. One type, the most common, has used unemployment and crime statistics and perhaps statistics relating to other matters as well. These are usually referred to as aggregate studies (they analyse statistical data in aggregated lumps) and sometimes employ quite complicated statistical techniques to manipulate the data. This is necessary because the researchers have probably had little control over how the data was collected in the first place, so statistical procedures are a way of introducing an element of control at a later stage. Despite their apparent sophistication such studies suffer from a number of shortcomings. To start with there is the problem of measuring crime and unemployment accurately and reliably. Officially recorded crime is not a true measure of crime; nor are official unemployment figures an accurate indication of the true level of unemployment. Several US studies use arrest rates as a measure of crime, whereas it is arguable that enforcement of the law might be influenced by economic conditions and by the incidence of unemployment. At least one researcher (Brenner 1976b) has used imprisonment rates as a measure of variations in the level of crime. This is completely inappropriate because, as we shall see later, it is possible that imprisonment rates may be affected by other processes within the system of criminal justice administration which are independent of the crime rate, but not unrelated to the impact of unemployment. In addition the way that unemployment and crime are measured can vary from time to time and from place to place: there have been nineteen changes in the way the unemployment figures for the UK are calculated since 1979 (Convery 1987).

However, there is often no alternative to using the data available despite its shortcomings. If one does this then certain pitfalls need to be avoided. For example, statistics have sometimes been cited showing that a high proportion of offenders are unemployed (e.g. Northumbria Police 1979, 1980: Appendices O and P). Whilst such information is of interest, for instance to those having to deal with large numbers of unemployed offenders, it is not evidence of a relationship between unemployment and crime. It is rather like saying that because most alcoholics drink tea, tea drinkers are more likely to become alcoholics. A further danger in drawing inferences from aggregate statistics is that of confusing offence rates with offenders. There may be no correlation between the level of crime in an area and the level of unemployment, and yet unemployed individuals may be more likely to commit offences than the employed. If there is a relationship between unemployment and crime, then it may be because more people are committing crimes, the number of crimes per person staying much the same, or a similar number of offenders may be committing more crimes.

Aggregate studies may be cross-sectional, comparing the levels of unemployment in different places with the levels of crime there. Not only do such studies face the problem of how unemployment and crime are measured, but the boundaries between these and other sets of statistics that have to be taken into account may not correspond with each other. An alternative type of aggregate study is the time series analysis, which takes unemployment and crime data over a period of years, controlling as far as possible for other factors, using statistical techniques. Harvey Brenner has used this approach, but his work has been criticized for its statistical inadequacies (Centre for Econometric Studies of the Justice System 1979; Winter 1982; Gravelle, Hutchinson, and Stern 1981). In particular Parker and Horwitz (1986) have analysed time series data allowing both for trend effects (the possibility that two variables are correlated over time simply because of similar trends in each variable) and the effects of time lag between unemployment and crime rates. They found that the strong relationship Brenner had observed was not apparent when such effects were controlled for. However, Parker and Horwitz only used data for a five-year period between 1974 and 1979, whereas Brenner had used data over a seventy-year period. The length of time over which data is analysed is important because if only short periods are used it is possible to select short term variations which become less apparent when a longer term perspective is taken. Thus, it is possible to identify, as Tarling (1982) does, periods when trends diverge. In this case Tarling refers to the upward trend in crime figures during the affluent 1960s. However, a long time period entails other problems, such as changes in the definition and measurement of phenomena over a period of years.

In what follows aggregate studies are referred to, but it is important to be aware of their limitations. In general a second, less common type of study is preferable: one which compares groups of actual people, offenders and non-offenders; employed and unemployed. Such studies still face problems. It may be difficult to get groups that are comparable. As with aggregate studies one can never be entirely certain that reported offending and unemployment are reliable, but they offer greater control over the information collected. Such studies are less common, however, because they are more time-consuming and expensive.

The influence of other factors

Apart from the considerations noted above, much of the discussion about the unemployment-crime link centres on the role played by other factors. Of these, the one that has attracted most attention is age. Mannheim (1940: 44) found that the relationship between unemployment and crime was least marked for the youngest age group: 'The elimination of the age groups under 21 thus has the effect of demonstrating the close conformity between the two sets of figures for the remainder of the population'.

The role of age in the relationship between the unemployment and crime has featured in several studies since Mannheim's. Unless data are broken down into age groups the effects of unemployment on crime tend to be obscured. This was demonstrated by two American researchers (Glaser and Rice 1959). An earlier writer, Vold (1958), had claimed that no clear associations could be shown to exist between economic conditions and crime. Glaser and Rice showed that once the data were analysed by age the significant relationship which Vold had failed to identify was found: 'We have presented evidence which suggests that more pronounced and consistent relationships between crime and economic conditions than were reported by previous studies can be obtained by using age-specific statistics' (1959: 685). Like Mannheim, what Glaser and Rice found was that the unemployment-crime link was strongest for the middle age ranges. Arrest data for juveniles (10–17 years) were less dependent on employment rates, suggesting that for these young people other, non-economic, factors are more important.

6

But this was only the beginning of interest in the topic. The age factor is important because the peak age for criminal convictions is the mid-teens, so a relationship of any kind between unemployment and crime in this age group will have considerable consequences for the crime figures. The *way* in which unemployment affects the young is also important since a number of different things are likely to be happening. On the one hand the youngest are not yet competing for jobs and hence are not directly affected by unemployment, whilst the next age group up, the school leavers, are particularly vulnerable to high unemployment because of the lack of vacancies. In addition, young people of various ages may be indirectly affected by unemployment through the effect it has on their family, friends, and the local community.

Hence Glaser and Rice's study has been followed by other attempts to investigate the age-crime-unemployment relationship in more detail. Gibbs (1966), for example, looked at Glaser and Rice's data and tried to explain why it was that unemployment and arrest rates were positively correlated between the ages of 19 and 34, but inversely related outside that age band. The mechanism he proposed he called status integration: the degree to which status occupancy in a population conforms to a particular pattern. He argued that if the majority of people in an age group are not in the labour force, as is the case with the old and the young, then unemployment does not deprive the individual of the means of achieving the cultural goals of that age group. Hence young people who are unemployed may be less likely to turn to crime because a high proportion of their peers are not working either, so unemployment *per se* has less effect on them. Although Gibbs produces further analysis of Glaser and Rice's data, which he claims supports his theory, it does not explain why the critical upper age is 40 or, indeed, take account of the crucial changes in social status that occur between 16 and 19. But Gibbs did draw attention to the need to take account of the extent to which various groups in the population differ in their rate of involvement in the labour market for reasons other than the availability of jobs. Gibbs also suggested, as have other commentators (e.g. Mannheim 1940 and Phillips, Votey and Maxwell 1972), that the relationship between crime and unemployment depends on social context.

Another researcher (Fleisher 1963) also sought to take Glaser and Rice's analysis a stage further, but he established that labour market conditions did have an effect on juvenile delinquency as well as on adult crime. He examined age-related crime data and presented evidence 'to suggest that factors associated with entering the labour market ... can help explain the age distribution of juvenile delinquency' (Fleisher 1963: 545). The effect of high unemployment on those entering the labour market is especially noticeable in the case of property offences. Fleisher then goes on to show that 'unemployment and arrests for property crimes are positively correlated, *regardless of age group*' (1963: 549, emphasis added). The outcome of Fleisher's study as a whole is the conclusion that: 'An examination of delinquency rates and other variables by age and through time suggests that the effect of unemployment on juvenile delinquency is positive and significant' (1963: 553). He ends by attempting to indicate the impact that high unemployment has on delinquency in human and economic terms. He estimates that a 100 per cent increase in unemployment over a given period results in a 25 per cent increase in the delinquency rate. If unemployment were to be reduced by half at any one time it would be accompanied by a decline in property crime of approximately 10 per cent and it was estimated that, at the time of the study, this would have meant a saving to the US economy of $100 million per annum.

Subsequent evidence on unemployment, age and crime has tended to support these conclusions. In this country Beeson (1965) found that parental unemployment was correlated with juvenile crime and McLintock (1976) suggests that there is a generation effect since the children of families where there is a history of unemployment are more likely to be delinquent.

Further evidence of the extent to which unemployment affects crime amongst the young comes from a study by Phillips, Votey and Maxwell (1972). Their research concentrated on four offences with an implied economic motive: larceny, burglary, robbery and car theft. They found that young people who were not working had higher crime rates than those who were. This is an important finding because of the methods used. Too often reference is made to the rate of unemployment amongst offenders; it is desirable, as was done here, to look at the offending rate among employed and unemployed people separately.

As well as looking at unemployment rates the study takes account of 'participation rates': that is, the proportion of the age group participating in the labour market. This is significant, as Gibbs (1966) recognized, because a lot of young people do not participate in the labour market. The study answers those who point to instances where crime rose during periods of affluence. It demonstrates

> the importance of participation rates relative to unemployment rates in explaining crime rates. This point is reinforced when one observes that during the middle and latter sixties, crime rates rose while unemployment rates declined. It is the decline in the participation rate which provides an explanation for the rise in crime during this period. (Phillips *et al.* 1972: 503)

Phillips *et al.* also examined data for white and black youth separately and found that unemployment increased crime in both ethnic groups: 'an increase in the unemployment rate and/or a decrease in the participation rate for either colour will increase the crime rate' (1972: 503). The strength of the analysis done by Phillips *et al.* is borne out by its success in predicting 'remarkably well' the crime and arrest rates for three years beyond the period used for estimation. They showed that labour market opportunities for the young had a strong effect on economically motivated youthful crime. The authors conclude 'that economic opportunity is the key factor in generating youthful crime ... that changing labour-market opportunities are sufficient to explain increasing crime rates for youth' (1972: 502). This study has been reported in some detail because of the importance of its conclusions and the methods by which they were reached. The authors' statement, 'We propose that our findings indicate that a successful attack on rising crime rates must consider the employment problems facing young people' (Phillips *et al.* 1972: 503), is not one that can be easily disregarded.

It is still true, however, that the study by Phillips *et al.* was carried out using aggregate, arrest rate data, entailing the shortcomings referred to earlier. Two more recent studies have been carried out in this country which involve groups of individual young offenders. The first was carried out in Northern Ireland in 1980 (Gormally, Lyner, Mulligan and Warden 1981). One hundred and twenty-three individuals between the ages of 16 and 18 who were referred to young offender institutions and probation teams in the province were interviewed. Details were sought concerning the periods when they were in work and full-time education or training, and when they committed offences. The individuals were about twice as likely to commit offences when they were not engaged in work, education or training as when they were. The possibility that those committing crimes most frequently were also the least employable was considered but discounted because it was found that employment had an effect on offending within the careers of particular individuals. It was concluded that: 'the experience of employment significantly slows down the rate of offending or, conversely, that the experience of unemployment leads to more crime' (1981: 18).

A study using a similar approach, in which each individual acted as his own control, was reported by Farrington, Gallagher, Morley, St Ledger and West in 1986. This used data on 411 individuals involved in the longitudinal Cambridge Study in Delinquent Development when they were between the ages of 14 and 18. This again showed that crime rates were higher during periods of unemployment than during periods of employment, particularly for offences involving material gain at ages 15–16, for the most delinquent youths and for youths who had lower status jobs when they were in employment. The study indicated that, because the relationship was strongest for those most predisposed towards offending, unemployment did not seem to cause basically law-abiding young people to commit crimes. School leaving itself was not, however, related to higher offending. Although published in 1986 this study, like a number of the others referred to here, is based on data collected some time previously, in 1971–2, at a time of lower unemployment generally. This is important because it may be that as unemployment becomes more normal in an age group, and incorporates individuals from a wider diversity of social backgrounds, the significance (and stigma?) of unemployment changes and so does the nature of the relationship with offending. Also, as Farrington *et al.* point out, it is unfortunate that similar studies have not been carried out using a wider age range.

In addition to age, a number of other factors also have to be taken into consideration when looking at the link between unemployment and crime. It has long been established that the incidence of crime correlates with various measures of social disadvantage (Mays 1963; Vinson and Homel 1965; McLintock 1976; Rutter and Madge 1976). This is true both for individuals and for communities. Poor housing, educational disadvantage, low income, poor health, and psychiatric problems are all found to be associated with a greater probability of conviction. They also correlate with unemployment. In recent years drug and alcohol use have been linked with both unemployment and crime (Collins 1982; House of Commons Official Report 1986; Parker 1986; Parker *et al.*, 1986). It therefore becomes difficult to distinguish the effects of one factor from another or to establish which causes which. The most reasonable conclusion on the evidence to date is that unemployment is a contributory factor, but that the causal link is not necessarily a simple one. What one is looking at is unemployment as an important determinant of the social conditions in which crime becomes more prevalent. Obviously the disappearance of unemployment would not mean the immediate disappearance of crime: crime has diverse origins. But the presence of unemployment may well play a role, along with other factors, in influencing the extent and pattern of particular offences. It is also possible that people from certain backgrounds and with certain problems, such as being out of work, are more likely to be caught for any offences they commit (see Stinchcombe 1963). It was the case, for example, that research in areas affected by the disturbances in the UK in October 1981 found that the unemployed reported having been stopped and searched by the police more frequently than the employed in the twelve months preceding the riots (Field and Southgate 1982).

A substantial study of the unemployment-crime link has been carried out by the Vera Institute of Justice in the United States (Sviridoff and McElroy 1985). This study is notable for having taken a broad approach to the issue, looking at it from different perspectives and using different methods of enquiry. The study looked not only at people who had committed crimes, but also at the communities in which crime, unemployment, and a variety of social problems occur. It suggested that a direct link between unemployment and crime is less clearly established than it was once thought to be, but that there are important indirect relationships between the extent and quality of employment and the extent and severity of income-related crime for particular groups. Like previous studies it recognized the importance of age but, unlike the study by Phillips, Votey and Maxwell referred to earlier, it found that the relationship between unemployment and crime was more marked for adults than young people. For those over 25 years old arrest rates were nearly twice as high in periods when they were not working as when they were. The most interesting comments, however, concern the impact of unemployment on local communities. It was suggested that the main effect of unemployment is to undermine and destabilize communities, and that this, in turn, produces high crime rates.

We may now identify some tentative conclusions. The first is that the relationship between unemployment and crime is by no means as simple and straightforward a matter as headline writers might lead one to suppose. Both unemployment and crime are hard to measure reliably. One must specify what crimes one is looking at, since there are considerable differences between being drunk and disorderly and commercial fraud, between rape and petty theft. One must also specify the age range involved and take account of the social context. The impact of unemployment may be different in a small rural community to what it is in an inner city area. Much may depend on what social provision and support structures are available to help offset the impact of unemployment. Because the studies that have been referred to vary widely in both what they studied (offences, samples, differences in when they were carried out etc.), and how they were done, the findings are not consistent and make it difficult to come to any general conclusions. The balance of the evidence seems to indicate that unemployment is indeed a factor which affects the likelihood of offending, but it is only one of a number of factors and it is necessary to specify the conditions in which the relationship is observed. Exactly how unemployment interacts with other factors is little understood as yet. Future research should perhaps place more

11

emphasis on the study of such interactions. Meanwhile there is insufficient consistent evidence to favour any one theory about how unemployment may be related to crime.

Unemployment and offenders

So far we have looked principally at the possible links between the economy, unemployment, and crime. But there is another perspective to be considered: the impact that unemployment has on offenders. The two perspectives are not, of course, entirely unconnected since, if known offenders are more likely to commit crimes if unemployed, and if unemployment rises, then this is an element in the link between levels of unemployment and crime. What we have in mind here is partly to do with offenders' chances of re-offending, but it is also to do with how offenders themselves are affected by unemployment and how they may be dealt with by others, such as sentencers, employers, and social workers. This is, as we said earlier, the forgotten perspective. But it is an important one. There is also a greater measure of agreement amongst the studies that have been carried out concerning such matters than is to be found amongst studies of unemployment and crime. This should, in theory, make the formulation of policy on such matters easier.

Over the years there have been a number of social and criminological studies of offenders and their characteristics (e.g. Davies 1969; Maxwell 1969; West and Farrington 1977 to mention but a few). These have often included information concerning offenders' employment, although the exact significance of the information has not always been made apparent: it has often featured as one of a number of descriptive variables on which information was sought. Other studies have, however, looked specifically at such matters as the effects of conviction on future employment, at unemployment and sentencing and at the help that might be available for unemployed offenders.

It has invariably been found that people known to have committed offences are more likely than others to be unemployed and this has been true even when unemployment generally was low. As unemployment has risen so the situation has got worse and this has affected, in various ways, the probation service, the courts and others who work with offenders. Unemployment has tended to be particularly acute among people who have been in prison (Maxwell 1969; Home Office, 1978), and unemployment among offenders has been found to be associated with other problems such as homelessness, alcoholism and mental disturbance (Tidmarsh, Wood, and King 1972; Banks and Fairhead 1976; Digby 1976). There is also evidence of a cycle of deter-

ioration in which unemployment, further offending and other difficulties tend to reinforce each other leading, for some people, to acute
multiple problems. As jobs become scarcer, so it becomes less
possible for a stable job to provide an opportunity for breaking
out of this cycle of deterioration. This is a particular source of
anxiety as far as young people are concerned. Although many
commit offences in their teens (Belson 1968) most cease to offend as
they reach their 20s. In the past this has tended to coincide with
getting a job, marrying and having a family. For an increasing
number of young people the first of these stabilizing and socially
acceptable life developments is no longer so easy to achieve. Studies
based on the Cambridge Study in Delinquent Development have
found that as the later teens are reached, peer influence declines
(West and Farrington 1977) and providing a young man marries a
non-delinquent woman a decline in offending is likely (West 1982).

Being convicted can have both immediate and longer term consequences for a person's employment. The most immediate consequence is the loss of a job following arrest and conviction (Martin
and Webster 1971; Corden, Kuipers, and Wilson 1978), although the
likelihood of this and the reasons for it vary. For example, stealing
from an employer, loss of driving licence and similar offences may
have a direct effect on one's employment. Receiving a custodial
sentence is also likely to result in the loss of a job, although sometimes employers will keep a job open for someone serving a short
sentence. A conviction also makes it much harder to get a job subsequently (Lowson 1970; Boshier and Johnson 1974; Corden 1976).

The consequences of conviction have not always been disastrous
for a person's employment prospects. Studies done in more affluent
times have shown that when jobs are plentiful offenders have a
reasonable chance of getting one. Much depends on the right circumstances and on support being available (Martin 1962; Martin and
Webster 1971; Soothill 1974). Those convicted of crimes tend to have
few skills and qualifications and have often been employed in
declining sectors of the economy. When such disadvantages are combined with a criminal record it is not surprising that, as unemployment has risen, so the problem of finding jobs for offenders has
become more acute. This tends to reinforce the cycle of deterioration
referred to above. Consideration of whether there is an alternative to
such a cycle leads one to look at how offenders are dealt with, what
provision is available for reversing the cycle, and what impact it has.
These are the matters to which we now turn, starting with how
unemployment affects the courts and sentencing.

Chapter two

Criminal justice and unemployment

Dealing with the workless

Dealing with the unemployed and with the consequences of unemployment is not new to the criminal courts. There is a strong historical link between the law and worklessness. In the past, courts have frequently found themselves dealing with people thrown into a life of poverty by social circumstances: the enclosures of the middle ages, the migration of populations during the industrial revolution, and the discharge of men from the army following the Napoleonic and other wars. The Vagrancy Acts of 1824–1935, parts of which are still in force today, had their origins in the Statute of Labourers of 1349. They were specifically directed at controlling surplus labour and contained references to 'idle and disorderly persons', 'rogues and vagabonds', and 'not having any visible means of support' (Home Office 1974). Engels, writing in the last century, saw the situation then as follows:

> But if a poor devil gets into such a position as involves appearing
> before the Justice of the Peace ... he is regarded from the
> beginning as guilty; his defence is set aside with a contemptuous
> 'Oh! we know the excuse,' and a fine imposed which he cannot
> pay and must work out with several months on the treadmill.
> And if nothing can be proved against him, he is sent to the
> treadmill nonetheless, 'as a rogue and a vagabond'.
>
> (Engels 1969: 306)

The direct links between the law and worklessness exemplified by the Vagrancy Acts have been underpinned by moral judgements about work and the ordering of society: worklessness has tended to be equated with fecklessness. This is apparent from the way criminal justice and penal policies have developed: work has often been seen as a necessary part of the penal and rehabilitative process. Hence the emerging prison system in the nineteenth century incorporated labour as an essential element (Ignatieff 1978). The preamble to an 1823 Act[1] regulating the prisons included the statement that 'the Classification, Inspection, regular Labour and Employment, and Religious and Moral Instruction, are essential to the Discipline of a Prison, and to the Reformation of Offenders'.

In more recent times, at least until a few years ago, there has been a belief that, for a person coming before the court, a job and a steady work record will count in his or her favour, whereas being out of work is an adverse reflection on character. Employment, a legitimate economic and social activity, has been seen as a factor which could be put into the scales of justice to help offset the illegitimate, anti-social activity for which a person was facing sentence. Hence a defendant's employment status and history have commonly featured in the personal information presented to the court, whether by a social enquiry report, a statement of 'antecedents' from the police, or a defence plea in mitigation. An article in *Justice of the Peace* (1982b: 700) expressed the general point: 'A man's (sic) employment situation has long been considered to be a relevant factor in sentencing.' But even during the period of low unemployment that prevailed until the mid-1970s, the level of joblessness was higher among offenders than among the population in general. A study of probation service clients in the late 1960s found that 40 per cent were unemployed (Davies 1969) and in the late 1970s, when unemployment nationally was just over 5 per cent, 40 per cent of all those coming before the courts were estimated to be unemployed (Gladstone 1979: 39). Even when jobs were available, offenders stood less chance than other citizens of getting one (Boshier and Johnson 1974).

During the present decade criminal justice agencies have been faced with a very different situation. Not only has the level of unemployment among offenders increased, with probation services reporting 80 per cent or more unemployment among clients (e.g. Greater Manchester Probation Service, 1986), but, in the worsening job market, it has been less tenable to assume that jobs would be available. Whether courts have recognized this is another matter. The *Justice of the Peace* (1982b: 700) reported a case where a defendant was threatened with a prison sentence unless he found work, and after an adjournment during which he managed to do so, the magistrate said: 'It just goes to show that those who have a real incentive to get work, like a threatened prison sentence, have little difficulty in getting a job.' This attitude may not be typical. But does courts' thinking change to allow for the fact that at times of high unemployment fewer offenders are able to offer a steady job as something that might count in their favour?

Certainly there is insufficient knowledge about employment in relation to offenders and criminal justice. For example, there are no readily available figures about the proportion of people who leave prison with no job to go to, and hence there is no sound basis for planning services for unemployed ex-prisoners. Some criminological studies have included information on offenders' employment histories, but often incidentally to other data. Studies looking specifically at employment and offenders (e.g. Martin 1962) are few indeed. And they are now dated, having been done at a time when the emphasis was on studying offenders' characteristics and when, because of high employment, being unemployed was regarded as a defect of the individual. There have been few attempts to assess more thoroughly the role played by work and employment in the modern criminal justice process and penal policy.

Unemployment and the prison population

Despite some innovations, imprisonment still lies at the heart of the penal system in this country, as in most others. Evidence from a number of studies shows that rising unemployment tends to be accompanied by rising numbers of people in prison. A considerable increase in imprisonment between 1820 and 1840 was largely attributed to a change in the nature of the labour market at the time, resulting from the growth of casual labour among agricultural workers and the breakdown of traditional master-servant relations in manufacturing (Ignatieff 1978, ch. 7). In a study of crime and unemployment between the First and Second World Wars, Mannheim (1940: 44) referred to the close similarities between the rate of unemployment and the number of prison inmates, and cited the report of the Prison Commissioners for 1922: 'It is probably right to say that unemployment is one of the chief contributory factors to the prison population of today.' Such observations have been supported in recent years by a number of quantitative studies. In the USA it was reported that 'The adult male prison population rises and falls as the unemployment rate rises and falls, allowing for a 15-month time lag before incarceration' (Ewing 1977: 2).

Brenner (1976a, 1976b) derived estimates of the impact of unemployment on incarceration rates from a study of data from the USA, Canada and the United Kingdom for a period of seventy years. He calculated that a 1 per cent increase in unemployment in the USA resulted in a 4 per cent increase in state prison admissions. In 1976 the United Nations Social Defence Research Institute (UNSDRI 1976: 14) concluded: 'The flow of referrals to deviance-oriented institutions (prisons, juvenile justice institutions, mental health institutions) rises steeply in periods of economic distress.' In the UK,

Gladstone (1979: 39) said: 'The number of youths aged 17 to 20 admitted to prisons and borstals in recent years seems to reflect the unemployment figures for late adolescence.' Figure 2.1 shows the average number of people in prison, and the average number officially regarded as unemployed, in England and Wales for each year between 1965 and 1985. Although the unemployment figures should be treated cautiously because of changes in counting rules, there are obvious similarities between the graphs, which tend to rise and fall together especially during 1969–79.

Now, although it looks persuasive, none of this material provides evidence of a causal link between unemployment and imprisonment. Indeed, there is an obvious possible explanation: if unemployment leads to more crime, surely this itself will lead to more people being imprisoned (assuming that the proportions of crimes cleared up and offenders dealt with remain much the same). However, a number of studies have taken this into consideration (Greenberg 1977; Jankovic 1977; Yeager 1979), and these have found that, even when the volume of offenders dealt with by the courts is taken into account, there remains a relationship between unemployment and imprisonment. In the USA:

Figure 2.1 Prison population and unemployment, 1966–86

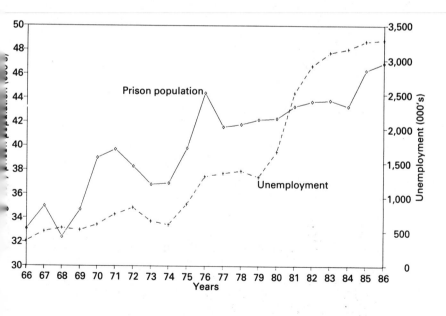

> High rates of commitment to prison during periods of
> unemployment ... cannot be explained as a passive judicial
> response to a larger caseload ... Changes in commitments to
> prison can be explained almost entirely by changes in the
> unemployment rate. Changes in the number of cases entering the
> criminal justice system and potentially available for
> imprisonment seem to be unimportant, as does the crime rate.
> (Greenberg 1977: 647–50)

Data for England and Wales have been thoroughly analysed by Box and Hale, who controlled for factors other than unemployment, and found a significant relationship: 'A simple way of reporting this result ... would be to say that, after controlling for other relevant factors, an increase of 1000 in the number of unemployed will lead, on the average, to 10 more people receiving prison sentences' (Box and Hale 1982: 28). The relationship was even more pronounced for young offenders, where Box and Hale estimated that for every 1000 increase in youth unemployment, 23 additional young males would be sent to prison.

It is worth highlighting certain points in what is known of the relationship between unemployment and imprisonment. First, the studies that have been done are consistent in concluding that there is such a relationship. This contrasts with research looking for links between unemployment and crime (and, indeed, much other research) where the findings are more diffuse and varied. Second, the relationship is not a recent phenomenon: the supporting evidence goes back many years. Third, the relationship is not confined to one country: it has been observed in several western ones, including the UK. Fourth, and most important, the relationship cannot be explained by changes in the numbers of people dealt with by the courts. Taken together these points suggest very strongly that, other things being equal, rising unemployment is likely to lead to an increase in the prison population. If this is true, the next question is: why?

Radical theorists have suggested that increasing use of imprisonment is a way of containing the unemployed and the social unrest stemming from unemployment (Quinney 1977). The UNSDRI report said: 'Under economic distress conditions social tolerance levels are lowered with regard to traditional forms of crime and deviance' (1976: 21). Box and Hale argued that:

> the growth of unemployment, which is itself a reflection of
> deepening economic crisis, is accompanied by an increase in the
> range and severity of state coercion, including the rate and length
> of imprisonment. This increased use of imprisonment is not a
> direct response to any rise in crime, but is an ideologically

motivated response to the perceived threat of crime posed by the swelling population of economically marginalised persons. (1982: 22)

But an alternative possible explanation is that unemployment restricts the options open to both courts and offenders, and this is elaborated below. Whatever the answer, these studies throw little light on it because they rely on aggregate data, comparing overall figures rather than specific cases, and thus offering no clues to the processes underlying the observed relationships. Consequently there is no potential for exploring changes of policy. The size of the prison population in recent years has caused much concern, and if high unemployment levels are a contributory factor it is important to consider what can be done in response. While reducing unemployment lies, by and large, outside the capacity of those who run the criminal justice system, there may be options for modifying criminal justice practice and policy which should be pursued.

Furthermore, many of the studies treat the prison population as a gross population, disregarding the fact that it depends both on the number of prisoners received and on the length of time they spend inside. It is thus not known whether the relationship between unemployment and the prison population comes about because in times of high unemployment (a) more people are sent to prison, although the length of incarceration remains much the same, or (b) the number of receptions remains fairly constant but people stay there longer, or (c) some mixture of (a) and (b). (For further explanation of the interaction between receptions and length of stay see Pease 1980).

Certain decision points can be identified in the criminal justice process at which a person's employment may be relevant:

(1)   Remand: the decision whether to keep a defendant in custody or release him or her on bail pending the outcome of the case. The Bail Act 1976, in giving and limiting the right to bail, refers among other things to the relevance of 'community ties', which may include a steady job.
(2)   Sentence: to what extent does the court take into account an offender's work status and record when deciding an appropriate sentence?
(3)   Parole: again, a prisoner's 'community ties', including work prospects, may be considered by a board in deciding early release.

The remand decision would affect mainly the number of receptions into prison, while the parole decision would affect only the length of time inside; the sentencing decision affects both.

Financial penalties

Although imprisonment is the penal sanction that attracts most attention, it is not the only one liable to be affected by changes in the level of employment. Indeed, until recently, certain ways of dealing with offenders have been closely linked to assumptions about the availability of paid employment for their effective operation. This is the case with financial penalties of any kind. The most common form of financial penalty is the fine, but courts are increasingly inclined to award compensation payments to the victims of crime, and may also order a convicted offender to contribute towards the costs of legal proceedings. For administrative convenience these different types of financial penalty are frequently referred to collectively as fines.

The fine is the most commonly used penalty in British courts. In 1981 a NACRO working party, chaired by Lady Howe, JP, published a report on fine default (NACRO 1981a) expressing support for the fine as a valuable non-custodial option for dealing with a

Figure 2.2 Decline of the fine, percentage of offenders fined for indictable offences

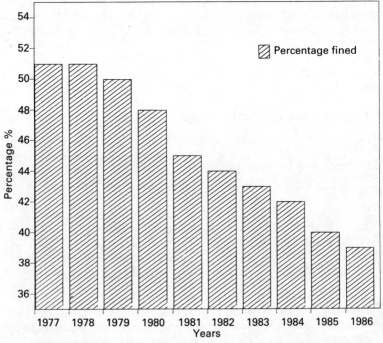

Source: Criminal statistics, 1986, Table 7.6

large number of offenders. The working party had become aware during its deliberations that courts were facing increasing problems in enforcing fines because of rising unemployment, but believed that the use of fines was something that should be safeguarded and sustained (para. 1.12). In view of this it is disturbing to note that the proportion of serious cases dealt with by a fine declined from around 50 per cent for most of the 1970s to 39 per cent in 1986 (Figure 2.2). Official comment has linked this decline in the use of fines to the rise in unemployment (Home Office 1984a: para. 7.17).

Several research studies in recent years have shown something of the extent to which the unemployed are, in the first instance, less likely to be fined and, when fined, are more likely to have difficulty in paying, and subsequently default. A Home Office study in 1978 found that unemployed offenders were significantly less likely to be fined than those who were employed (Softley 1978). Instead, it was suggested, some received discharges or probation, others a custodial sentence. The same study indicated that for some the attempt to pay a fine caused significant hardship and meant not paying other bills. A later study found a strong relationship between courts' rates of committal to prison for default and local unemployment rates, and 60 per cent of those committed were unemployed (Moxon 1983). Another study showed that a high proportion of defaulters had little or no chance of paying and had a term of imprisonment imposed to be served in default (Softley 1983). A Scottish study also found that default was greater among the unemployed and that a large proportion of defaulters were living on low incomes, many at subsistence level, and were having difficulties in making ends meet, even for essentials such as housing, fuel and food (Millar 1984).

The practical dilemma facing the courts can be readily imagined. It is likely to be acute in the more serious type of case where the bench, having determined that a fine is the appropriate penalty, feel it must be a heavy one to mark the gravity of the offence. But they are also required to have regard to the means of the offender (Magistrates' Courts Act 1980: s.35), and if the offender is unemployed what are the chances of a fine being paid? The dilemma is not entirely new since, as noted earlier, unemployment among offenders has always been above the average, but the significance of recent developments is that (a) in sheer numerical terms the problem is now greater, and (b) whereas in the past a bench may have felt that a person could obtain a job to pay a fine, this is no longer so often the case.

Growing unemployment thus raises a number of questions about financial penalties. How are courts responding to the dilemma? Is one answer simply not to impose fines on the unemployed, but to use other sanctions? What are the implications for the awarding of compensation – something that is increasingly felt to be desirable in the interest of the victim? Should community service orders be used for people unable to pay their fines? Should the option of payment by 'attachment of earnings' be extended to allow the unemployed to pay by 'attachment of benefit'? Should Britain copy several European countries by introducing a 'day-fines' system, in which the court fixes the fine as a number of units appropriate to the offence, and administrators translate this into money terms according to the offender's means?

Imprisonment of fine defaulters is unlikely to explain the reported association between unemployment and the prison population, for two reasons. First, fine defaulters spend relatively short periods in prison. Although they comprise just under a quarter of all prison receptions, they are only about 3 per cent of the prison population, which would thus be only marginally affected by even a large increase in the number of defaulters going to prison. Second, because the overall use of fines appears to decline as unemployment grows, so the number of receptions for default is likely to decline, even though

Figure 2.3 Prison receptions for fine default, 1966–86

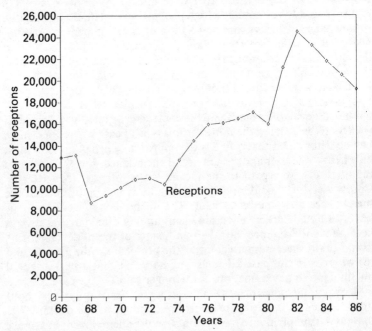

Source: Prison statistics, England and Wales, 1966–86

Figure 2.4 Receptions per 1,000 male offenders fined 1976–86

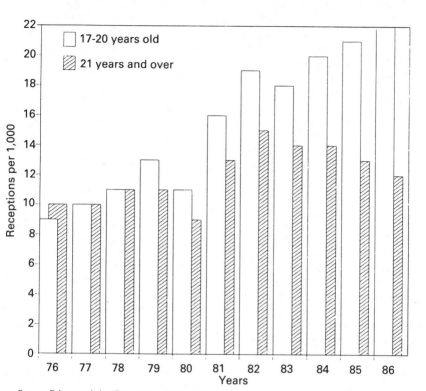

Source: Prison statistics, England and Wales, 1986

the unemployed who are fined may be more susceptible to default. In fact this has happened in recent years: the number of receptions for fine default has dropped since 1982 (Figure 2.3). The decrease may be due to several factors (in 1986, for example, there was a decline resulting from changes in the law) but in recent years the decline in the use of the fine is especially likely to be one of them. Of particular concern, however, is the marked rise in the proportion of 17–20 year olds fined who have been imprisoned for default (Figure 2.4).

Probation

Probation officers have generally given consideration to the employment status and prospects of their clients, whether they are on probation orders, statutory licences, or voluntary after-care. Information about a person's employment history usually features in the social enquiry reports that the probation service prepares for the courts. Courts' traditional regard for the work ethic is reflected in the words which, at least until recently, were used (with slight variations) in many courtrooms to explain to an offender his or her obligations under a probation order: 'To be of good behaviour and lead an industrious life; to inform the probation officer at once of any change of residence or employment' (Richman and Draycott 1984: 7555); and the probation officer, under the time-honoured duty to 'advise, assist and befriend', was expected among other things to encourage the probationer to get or keep a steady job.

In the last twenty years or so probation officers' methods of working with their clients have changed and diversified. As well as the traditional casework based on individual counselling sessions, probation services now do much work with offenders in groups organized for specific purposes. There are groups for educating alcohol abusers; for discussing and confronting offending behaviour; for learning social skills and survival skills like budgeting and house-keeping. Services run probation and bail hostels, day centres and drop-in centres. They are involved in schemes for offering basic education and for advising people on matters like housing and welfare rights. Participation in some of these arrangements is sometimes made a condition of probation by the court. These and other developments are described by several authors in a collection of papers edited by Harding (1987). Coincident with the last few years of these changes has been the rise in unemployment, whose significance for probation work has been recognized in surveys and reports prepared by individual services (e.g. Greater Manchester Probation Service 1986) and by the Conference of Chief Probation Officers. [2] These surveys show that in many areas now the great majority of people on probation caseloads are unemployed, and that many of them are long-term unemployed for whom the prospects of getting work are very poor. The Greater Manchester Probation Service report (1986: 13), for example, says: 'For many clients unemployment will be a recurring problem and for some a more prolonged, possibly even permanent experience.' In this changed climate, what do courts expect of probation officers in regard to the employment of offenders with whom they are concerned? There are several aspects of current practice on which information is lacking. It is not known, for example, whether unemployed people are more likely than others to be the subject of social enquiry reports; nor whether officers recommend the unemployed more frequently for probation orders or for longer ones; nor whether, in cases where the sentence does not accord with the SER recommendation, employment status has made any difference. Nor is there much systematic information on how probation officers work with the unemployed offenders they supervise, and whether their practices vary in different parts of the country with differing experiences of unemployment.

Community service orders

Community service orders (CSOs) are an important penalty to consider in the present context, for two reasons. First, they involve work. Second, they were introduced in the early 1970s, a time of virtually full employment. So it is appropriate to examine what impact rising unemployment may have had on this peculiarly work-oriented form of sentence. The introduction of CSOs resulted from a report of the Advisory Council on the Penal System (Home Office 1970). The section dealing with community service makes no mention whatever of employment (and this even when 40 per cent of probationers were said to be unemployed). The emphasis is on the reformative value of the measure (para. 35) and its value in the treatment of the young offender (para. 38). It is noted in passing that the work would be carried out in the offender's leisure time (para. 39).

Courts' use of CSOs has greatly increased in the past ten years or so, from 2,600 or 0.6 per cent of those sentenced for indictable offences in 1975 to 33,800 or 8 per cent in 1985. In the second half of this period unemployment has also grown, and the question arises of how courts are using CSOs in the new situation. One observer commented: 'CSO is not intended as a sort of job for the unemployed ... he should not be given more hours than he would otherwise have been just because he is unemployed' (Samuels 1982: 644). Much has been written about CSOs, but research has mainly focused on their operation as a penal sanction. A study in Northern Ireland (Jardine, Moore, and Pease 1983) found that unemployed offenders were being given longer orders than other people, but this may not be typical of the rest of the UK. There has been no systematic information on whether being unemployed affects the likelihood of receiving a CSO. If it does, this relationship may become entangled with the issue of whether or not CS should be used only as an alternative to imprisonment, a topic of much debate.

The growth of CSOs has made considerable demands on the probation service, who organize the system and find places for offenders ordered to perform work. The rise in unemployment has seen a large development of special employment schemes, both voluntarily and officially sponsored, whereby participants work to benefit the community, the biggest being the Community Programme. A survey in 1981 found a lack of co-ordination between different types of community service work (National Youth Bureau 1981). In this context the penal sanction of CSOs, and the resources required to provide it, need further study.

Deferment of sentence

Courts have the power to defer passing sentence for a time to see whether the offender will fulfil a specific expectation. Nott and Corden (1980), a studying deferment by courts in West Yorkshire, found that:

> Expectations in relation to employment or school attendance were most often stated in court; there was a high level of unemployment among the offenders on deferment, and the sentencers clearly placed a high value on work as a stabilising influence in offenders' lives. On sentence, however, courts used the avoidance of further offences as the main justification of a non-custodial penalty, which may reflect a recognition by some sentencers that at a time of unprecedentedly high unemployment, only very limited improvements in this area could be expected.

The study did not show whether unemployed offenders were more likely than others to have their sentences deferred, and there has been little other research carried out on this power of the courts.

A framework for research

Enough has been said to show the desirability of further research into how courts are dealing with offenders at a time of high unemployment. This would not address all questions about unemployment and the criminal justice system; for instance, parole would not be included, nor would policing. (The possibility that unemployed offenders are more likely than others to be caught and charged is suggested by the finding of Smith (1983) that in London unemployed men had a higher chance of being stopped and questioned, and of being arrested.) But interest in the topics so far discussed – courts' attitudes to the workless, the relationship between unemployment and imprisonment, the implication of unemployment for fines and other penalties, and (to some extent) for the probation service – gave rise to the research on magistrates' courts which is described below and in the next chapter. It was hoped by comparing individual cases to throw more light on relationships between unemployment and court decisions than is available from aggregate data; and by observing court proceedings, and discussing issues with key people concerned in them, to understand better the processes involved.

The possibility of discriminatory social attitudes on the part of magistrates could not be ruled out. But it was postulated that another plausible explanation might be found in the way that unemployment restricts options: courts' sentencing options in particular, but also offenders' options in being able to put before the courts positive, persuasive arguments to mitigate their sentences. Thus the emphasis was more on a process of criminal justice decision-making than on social attitudes and structures in general. This is not to deny the validity of other theoretical approaches but, in so far as it was hoped that the study would yield lessons about practice and policy, the aim was to find out whether mechanisms were operating that were susceptible to change: for example, by introducing new elements which would re-open options.

Refinements were needed to allow for variations in courts' experiences of unemployment and also in their sentencing practices. First, unemployment is distributed unevenly over the country. Some areas have had to live with high unemployment for a considerable time, and may have made adjustments that had not yet emerged in other places where high unemployment was a more recent experience, or where unemployment was still comparatively low. It was not possible to go back in time to study the changing impact of unemployment, but it was feasible to compare areas with different histories and experiences of it (i.e. to do a cross-sectional study). It was surmised that in an area of relatively low unemployment some of the traditional expectations about defendants getting work might persist, whereas in areas where unemployment was chronically high courts might have adapted to this situation, placing less weight on employment matters as a result. The hypothesis does, therefore, take account of the part that might be played by social attitudes. It may be expected to apply most forcefully to the use of custodial sentences, but is also valid with regard to others, such as the fine. However it does not easily take account of other developments that may have been occurring in criminal justice during the period that unemployment has been increasing. For example, a shift in policy away from the 'treatment' model towards a 'just deserts' approach may mean that social information about offenders, including their employment history, is now accorded less weight than it was previously.

Second, past research had demonstrated the importance of what is called 'the tradition of the bench' (Hood 1972; Tarling and Weatheritt 1979). Magistrates' courts, even some neighbouring ones, tend to show a robust amount of independence and individuality in the ways they work, including their approaches to sentencing. It may therefore be that benches with different traditions and sentencing patterns respond to higher unemployment in different ways. These considerations shaped the design of the research project so as to take account of both regional variations in the experience of unemployment and the sentencing tradition of the bench.

So the general hypothesis for the study may be stated as follows. There is a strong historical link between the criminal justice system and the work ethic. But as increasing numbers of offenders appearing before the courts are unable to offer their employment in mitigation, so the courts are less able to take this into consideration in arriving at decisions. The implication is thus not so much that courts are punishing offenders for being out of work, but that they are presented with a situation in which options are curtailed and reduced for all concerned (offender, probation service, and court). One may further expect the response of courts to be conditioned to some extent by their sentencing traditions and the experience of unemployment in their area.

From the general hypothesis were derived a series of specific ones which may be summarized as follows:

(i)   Employment information is important to courts in making decisions on offenders, but less so than information on offending and criminal history.

(ii) Other things being equal, unemployed offenders are less likely than the employed to be dealt with in certain ways (financial penalties, also bail), and more likely to be subjected to others (probation, CSO, custody).

(iii) Unemployed offenders are likely to receive different amounts or lengths of such penalties from the employed.

(iv) Social enquiry reports are more likely to be written on unemployed offenders, and to recommend some disposals rather than others.

(v)   The importance of employment in court decisions, and the hypothesized disparities in decisions between employed and unemployed, will vary depending on the local experience of unemployment and on the sentencing tradition of the court.

Research design and methods

During 1984–6 the NACRO Research Unit carried out a study designed to test these hypotheses. Ideally it should have included Crown Courts as well as magistrates' ones, but resources did not stretch to this. Also it was thought there might be difficulties of access, as other researchers had found in attempting to study Crown Court sentencing (Ashworth, Genders, Mansfield, Peay, and Player

1984). So the research was confined to a small but carefully selected number of magistrates' courts in England and Wales.

Three areas were selected to represent different employment conditions. The North-East of England was chosen as an area with historically high levels of unemployment, where it may be supposed that courts were used to dealing with an above average proportion of unemployed offenders. By contrast, the South-East was selected as an area where, even during the recent economic recession, unemployment had been lower than elsewhere. London was excluded, however, because of both the wide variation of employment conditions in different parts of the capital and the rather different nature of London courts. Finally, the West Midlands was chosen as an area which had recently undergone a transition from relative affluence and low unemployment to severe recession and high unemployment.

Within each of these three areas a pair of courts was chosen for their contrasting sentencing practices. A sentencing tradition may incorporate many elements but the most commonly used, if somewhat crude, indicator of it is the court's proportionate use of custody. So one court was chosen for having, over several years, a custody rate below the local average, while the other's was above this average. The result was to place the six courts in a 3 × 2 design, as represented in Figure 2.5.

Figure 2.5   Research design, unemployment and the courts

	Unemployment		
Use of Custody	Low	High	Low→High
Below average	Court L1	Court H1	Court LH1
Above average	Court L2	Court H2	Court LH2

Figures A1 and A2 in the Appendix are graphs of the unemployment rates for the localities of the courts, and of their custodial sentencing rates, and show that the six indeed met the criteria.[3]

The study focused on adult offenders (i.e. those aged 17 and over), and at each of the courts the research was carried out in three main ways. First, information was extracted from case records of a sample of over 500 men (aged 17 upwards) who had been sentenced for property offences – mostly burglary, theft and criminal damage – between 1983 and 1985.[4] The information comprised mainly details of the man's offence and criminal record, his employment status on the day of sentence, the recommendation of the social enquiry report if there had been one, and the sentence itself. This information was analysed by multivariate statistical techniques to see whether there was any tendency for employed and unemployed men to receive different treatment, after allowance had been made for any differences between them in the seriousness of their offending and past criminal history. Property offences were chosen because (a) they comprise about 70 per cent of the indictable cases dealt with by magistrates, (b) it was thought that any links between unemployment and court decisions might be clearer there than with other types of crime, and (c) offending seriousness could be more easily measured and controlled for. This variable, together with past criminal record, was taken into account by means of an 'offending score', which combined seven items describing the current offending and past criminal record into a single measure. The analyses of the records data were the main basis for deriving findings on patterns of sentencing and on the use of social enquiry reports. A small additional analysis was done on information from the payment records of men who had been fined, to see whether employment status bore on the likelihood of default.

Second, the researchers sat in each court watching and listening to the cases of over 50 defendants (of both sexes, aged 17 and over) at remand stages, and at least 65 at the sentencing stage. It was not possible to choose these samples systematically like the records ones, but minor motoring cases were largely avoided, and each sample contained a sufficient variety to facilitate a broad picture of that court's practice. The focus was on observing what information was given to the court about the defendant, by whom and when, and how employment fitted into it. Documents handed to the bench were seen afterwards. The observations provided data not otherwise available, like mitigation argument; amplified some of what was in the records, like employment histories; and assisted an understanding of the processes leading to the decisions of the bench.

Third, semi-structured interviews were held with at least eight key personnel at each court, including: the chairman and a deputy; the justices' clerk and a deputy; the senior probation officer and a court team probation officer; a prosecuting solicitor and a defence solicitor. The purpose was to obtain their perspectives on how unemployment might affect the ways in which the court made decisions. Topics included: perceptions of local unemployment; its significance for the work of the court; the bearing of a defendant's employment status and history on the court's consideration of his or her case and of particular sentences; awareness of local work schemes; local crime problems; and any particular court practices and policies.

The researchers spent two months at each court. As well as the records, observations and interviews, opportunities were taken for informal discussion with court staff, some fine enforcement sessions were watched, and local background material was collected. Towards the end of the study interim findings were presented at a seminar to key informants from the courts, whose comments were taken into account in the final synthesis of the results.

Technical aspects of the research method, and statistical and other results, have been reported in detail elsewhere (Crow and Simon 1987). In the next chapter, following a description of the courts, the main findings of the study are considered in the context of the ideas and hypotheses discussed above.

Notes

1 Act for consolidating and amending the Laws relating to the building, repairing and regulating of certain Gaols and Houses of Correction in England and Wales, 1823. 4 Geo. IV, C. 64.
2 Now the Association of Chief Officers of Probation.
3 The choice of courts was based on an examination of local unemployment rates for 1979–84, sentencing statistics for 1979–83, population figures, and maps of administrative boundaries, very small rural courts being excluded. Access negotiations were assisted by the Home Office, the Magistrates' Association, and the Justices' Clerks Society; the Association of Chief Police Officers and the Association of Chief Officers of Probation were also informed of the research. Six courts (from a short list fitting the criteria) gave the researchers all facilities requested. A seventh court in Wales served as a pilot.
4 For the sampling period (which varied depending on the size of the court) every case was taken except those of men fined, of which every second one was taken and then weighted by two in most analyses. This yielded an 'augmented sample' of over 500 from each court. Table A1 in the Appendix shows that the six samples fitted the research design. For full details see Crow and Simon (1987).

Chapter three

Unemployment and magistrates' courts

The courts and their surroundings

Both the courts studied in the South-East, the L courts, were in areas of apparent affluence. L1 served a town of about 50,000 people, with surrounding villages and farms. Formerly a market town, it had developed since the 1960s and was still expanding, with an unemployment rate less than half the national average. A variety of light industries and service occupations flourished, and people from London had moved in to join the established local population. Consequently home ownership, and house prices, were high. The magistrates' court had recently been enlarged to incorporate two small rural ones, and occupied a modern building, but the courtroom atmosphere seemed still to have something of the market town rather than of an urban centre. L1 was the smallest of the six courts studied. Crime was not thought to be a particularly severe problem locally, though public disorder in the town centre in the late evening caused some concern. There was also a larger than usual number of motoring cases because of the town's situation on a popular route between the South-East and the Midlands.

Court L2 served a heavily built-up town with 100,000 inhabitants, the centre of a buoyant economy. Much employment was focused on a large trading estate with many industrial and commercial firms, of which some were long established but had modernized and expanded, and others had moved in to join the growing prosperity. Some large companies and offices were located in the town centre. Unemployment was well below the national average, and was largely attributed to a mismatch between vacancies and the skills of job seekers, as older manufacturing industries had given way to high technology and service occupations. As in L1, home ownership and house prices were high, but L2 was more mixed socially, and overcrowding was among the worst outside London. The thriving modern shopping centre, which the local council was determined to shield from competition, attracted custom from a wide area. At the magistrates' court business was conducted in an atmosphere of brisk efficiency. The bench were particularly concerned to deter shoplifting and to deal with what they felt was an increasing problem of violence; there was also concern about misuse of drugs and alcohol.

In the two North-Eastern centres, H1 and H2, the scene was very different. The researchers were told of streets where virtually no one had a job, where people had been out of work for years, and where for many the only realistic chance of legitimate occupation was a place on a government scheme. The problem was invariably described by words like 'appalling'. Court H1 served two distinct areas. One was a cluster of villages, with a total population of about 35,000, where traditional heavy industry and coal mining had gone and nothing had replaced them. Family ties and local loyalties were strong, and most residents had resigned themselves to chronically high unemployment. Over half lived on council estates and there was no scarcity of houses. The other area was a new town development whose population had grown since the early 1970s to about 55,000. Although a great deal of effort had been put into attracting employers to the newly built factories and pleasant housing, early hopes had been badly hit by the recession of the 1980s. Some families had moved in, but their aspirations had not been fulfilled, and among the consequences was a high incidence of young families, single parents, and domestic and social problems. Court H1 had a reputation for granting legal aid more than many others and for a lenient sentencing policy. In the older part of its catchment area crime was petty and predictable, though there was some concern about the growth of burglary and the proximity of a major trunk road gave rise to a number of motoring offences. In the area of the new town criminals, often from outside, had been attracted to the middle-class houses and new industrial premises, and the large shopping centre suffered from theft.

Court H2 served a population of about 200,000 in one of the towns whose names have become almost synonymous with unemployment, as traditional industries have ceased to exist. Even so there was a reluctance to move away from long established community ties. There was no real shortage of housing, though some of the older council dwellings were uninviting, in great grim blocks which dominated parts of the town. The court had a local reputation for toughness, though in fact its custodial sentencing rates for adults was near the national average. Proceedings were conducted with a straightforward 'no nonsense' air. Crime was seen as a problem in the area generally, with particular concern about the level of burglary and car theft, and about disturbances in the town centre on weekend evenings.

The areas surrounding the two West Midlands courts, LH1 and LH2, had suffered more recently from the recession, moving from boom to slump in a relatively short period with considerable loss of jobs. LH1, the largest of the six courts, served a city of some 300,000 people, where many jobs had gone from manufacturing industries. There was a long council house waiting list and many dwellings, council and privately owned, needed repairs. The court, in spite of its size, had an atmosphere of informality. There was much concern about local violent crime, the rising incidence of house burglaries, and drunkenness and disorder in the city centre.

Court LH2 was situated in a densely-populated part of the West Midlands conurbation, serving an area of about 150,000 people. Local engineering and metal manufacturing firms had collapsed in the recession leaving many areas of derelict land. Once again the housing stock, half of it council-owned, was in need of repair; many young families lived in high-rise blocks. At the court the general atmosphere was courteous but firm: in the words of one solicitor, 'the magistrates know where they're going'. They expressed concern about violent crime and vandalism, theft of cars and scrap metal, and theft in the shopping centre. Informants at both the LH courts spoke of the difficulties local people were having in adapting to changed circumstances and frustrated expectations, and of the growing prevalence of debt.

Attitudes to the unemployed

All the courts were conscious of changing times. Many interviewees, including magistrates and court staff, welcomed the opportunity to discuss local economic conditions and the problems they felt were being caused for the court's work. Often they began by speaking of financial penalties, which are discussed below. But it was clear, from what they said and from cases observed, that attitudes differed between courts.

Both the L courts, though agreeing that unemployment had increased, showed much of the traditional belief that offenders ought to be in work. Indeed many were: the proportion of unemployed men in the records samples was below 50 per cent, and of the people observed at sentence the majority were employed and few of the unemployed had been so for longer than a few months. Magistrates felt that, except for people with obvious handicaps, 'anyone who seriously wants a job will get a job', and that some lacked motivation and discipline. Both courts, especially L2, sometimes fined unemployed offenders in terms which made it clear that they were expected to get a job.

In the town of L1 the work ethic seemed particularly strong. At the court magistrates were sympathetic to the problems of some young people, but felt that employment was a stabilizing influence which they needed and, with persistence, could obtain. The L1 attitude was perhaps summed up in the remarks a bench chairwoman made to one young woman: 'Are you trying to get work? Not very hard? You do your best to get a job. It's not easy but it's not impossible.' At L2 there were fewer remarks in the courtroom, but the attitudes conveyed by senior magistrates and their clerk in interviews were robust and traditional. A defendant's plea of having 'a job to start on Monday' would not carry much weight, but his employment history would be taken as a pointer to stability and character, or lack of them. In discussing the use of custodial sentences the chairman said,

> If a person lives in a regular address, has got a wife and family, you would hesitate to send him to prison unless it really was for the protection of the public. Quite obviously if a chap was footloose, doesn't work regularly, he must be a candidate to go.

But a prosecutor at L2 said that in fact the court was more sympathetic to the unemployed than it had been five years ago. At L1 a solicitor's comments suggested that magistrates had reacted to rising unemployment with some concern and puzzlement: 'It's almost like a cloud passing over the sun.'

At the H courts the workless offender was accepted as the norm. In the records samples at least two-thirds of the men were unemployed, and others were described as 'permanent sick' though in better times some of them might have found jobs. The majority of people observed at sentence were workless, many having been so for at least a year. Very few showed any hope of getting work or training. The small number with a CP or YTS place were more optimistic, but others with this experience already behind them had had no work afterwards. Court clerks in enquiring into defendants' means took it for granted that most were living on social security and, as described below, fines were geared to the supplementary benefit rate.

The chairman of the H1 bench described local unemployment as appalling. In the old days, he said, to be out of work was 'a most disgraceful thing' but nowadays the community accepted it. Some magistrates were unemployed. Interviewees said that for an offender a real job was 'like gold dust' and that the bench would 'bend over backwards' to protect it: thus there would be a tendency for some employed offenders to receive more lenient treatment. Magistrates showed great concern for the problems of the unemployed, and for the prospects of young people growing up without work. At H2, by contrast, the court's attitude seemed much more matter-of-fact.

Unemployment was normal and offending had to be dealt with; so offenders were sentenced in a straightforward manner with apparently little heed paid to distinctions in work status. Magistrates and staff were firmly of the opinion that a person's job would make no difference to the sentence (except perhaps sometimes to the amount of a fine), and the chairman said that a defendant's attitude to work could not be taken into account because there would be no evidence to support it. Two cases were observed where a dramatic defence plea for a non-custodial sentence, on young men who had managed against all odds to get work, did not succeed. But some informants thought that very occasionally employment status might influence the court's decision.

People at the LH courts were well aware of the worsening local economy. The proportions of unemployed in the research samples were as high as at the H courts, but on the whole they had not been out of work for so long. A few others were self-employed people whose businesses were in difficulties. Magistrates and court staff said that many people, especially the young, were having problems in adjusting to reduced incomes and modifying their expectations of a material standard of living which a few years previously they had taken for granted. At LH1 consideration for the unemployed was shown mainly in relation to financial penalties: the unemployed were given longer to pay and a very few had outstanding fines remitted. No remissions were observed at any of the other courts.

Magistrates at LH2 seemed to be struggling to come to terms with the changed situation. They felt frustration at being unable to impose what they judged to be realistic fines, and increasingly turned to other penalties, especially community service orders, as discussed below. Although they said that a job was no longer such an expected 'badge of respectability' other informants suggested that this view was modified by an age distinction: an older man made redundant after a steady record of employment with a well-regarded local firm would receive more sympathy from the court than a youth who said there was no point in looking for work. The observers noticed that in both the LH courts advocates for unemployed offenders often mentioned their hopes of work; this suggests that a lingering work ethic was still thought to influence bench decisions. But a solicitor at LH2 said the court's attitude to unemployment had changed, though more recently than at some other places.

Thus it seemed that the six courts' attitudes to the unemployed varied according to their local experiences and their own sentencing customs, the work ethic being most apparent still at the L courts where unemployment was lowest, and lingering at LH2, the 'transitional' court with a relatively high use of custody. Interwoven with this pattern was the factor of age: young offenders who had a criminal record, but not much chance to acquire a work record, were likely to present less well than an older person who had a work record to trade on.

Although the research focused on the consequences of unemployment for courts' decisions about offenders, interviewees often mentioned unemployment in the wider context of social problems with which they were locally familiar. They expressed concern that so many young people were growing up with little or no experience of regular employment, and felt that this was having an adverse effect on their attitudes to work and society, including the law and the courts. The research did not set out to study whether unemployment contributed to crime, but interviewees frequently raised this spontaneously as an issue and, while views were mixed, some people at the H and LH courts believed that recent experience suggested a connection. In these areas also it was commonly said that there was a growing incidence of family problems, divorce, and other social troubles which were attributed to rising unemployment. It was noticeable that at four of the six courts there were reports of regular town centre disturbances and concern about what was perceived as the growing level of drunkenness, although respondents were reticent about ascribing such problems to unemployment, pointing out that many of those dealt with for offences ensuing from such behaviour did have jobs.

Information for the bench

Information is the food of decision-making. One of the researchers' first concerns was to examine the weight attached by court personnel to information about defendants' employment. How important was this in relation to other matters? What were its sources, how much was given and at what stages in the court proceedings? Although it was the focus of study, the particular topic of employment can be seen as exemplifying the broader general issue of the role of information in the court process. The availability and presentation of personal information are crucial to the picture of the defendant that emerges during the few moments for which he or she stands before the magistrates.

Little personal information, on employment or anything else, was offered about defendants who appeared at remand stages before being tried. It had been hypothesized that employment matters might in some cases affect decisions about bail, but in fact employment was hardly ever mentioned. Usually the magistrates heard only the prosecutor's outline of the offences charged; even the existence or otherwise of a defendant's criminal record was not often revealed. Because of the Bail Act 1976, which legislated for a presumption in favour of remand on bail, most defendants, except those facing very grave charges, were readily granted bail with few questions asked. In doubtful cases police objections to bail, usually based on the nature of the alleged offence and the defendant's past criminal behaviour, weighed far more than anything else, and defence solicitors' arguments for bail were mainly concerned with minimizing such matters. At post-conviction stages when an offender was remanded (for the court to get a social enquiry report, or other information like a driving record) the bench usually knew rather more about him or her, but even then employment matters were very seldom part of any plea for bail, which was nearly always granted (or withheld) to continue the existing state of affairs. Altogether, in the total of 573 observed remands (from all six courts) a fully-argued bail application was made in only 51, and in only 11 of these (from five courts) was employment information a substantial part of the case. The most frequent of these arguments was that the defendant would lose his job, or place on an employment scheme, if kept in custody. Three of these 11 applications succeeded.

The impression given by the observations was very similar at each of the six courts. In interviews some probation officers and solicitors thought that having a job would help a defendant in a bail application, to the extent that it reflected 'community ties' like having a fixed address and a family. It may be that in some of the observed cases employment would have been more often mentioned if more of the defendants had been employed. It is also possible that at courts serving populations in some other areas, with a higher proportion of transients, evidence of community ties would feature more in bail applications. But findings from the six courts in this study gave practically no support to the hypothesis that bail is less likely for defendants who lack jobs.

Sentencing is a different matter. At this stage a bench often has for consideration a variety of information about the offender: not only the nature and circumstances of the offending, and his or her past criminal record if any, but also personal details – family, employment, health and so on. Employment is only part of the total picture that the court sees (and it may feature more prominently in some cases than others). In interviews all informants stressed that the bench would, first and foremost, consider the offending behaviour and the offender's previous criminal record if any; but many said that after these matters some importance would generally be attached to employment.[1] This was borne out in the analyses of the records samples which, as explained on pp. 46–7, showed that sentencing was generally related to employment status but much less strongly than it was to offending. Thorpe (1978) found that magistrates offered a variety of items would usually look at offending and record first, and employment second. Therefore, and given the focus of the study, it was reasonable for the researchers, in looking at information presented to the bench, to concentrate on employment matters, while placing them in the context of all the information the magistrates received. The findings may be considered under several heads: the sources and amounts of information, and the ways in which it was presented and used.

Sources and amounts

For many offenders a major source of information was of course a social enquiry report. These were obtained mainly in the more serious cases, and more often for offenders under 21 than older ones. But there were other variations too. The H courts, especially H2, called for SERs less frequently than the other four, most of the difference occurring with men over 21. After allowing for offending scores it was found that LH1 got SERs rather more often for unemployed men than employed ones in the younger age group, while the L courts and LH2 showed this tendency for the older men but not the younger. Thus, to some extent, each court had its own pattern of use, and the L and LH courts gave some support to the hypothesis that SERs would be used more for the unemployed.

Social enquiry reports, when available, were very often the fullest source of information on employment status and history, as well as other personal matters. A more frequent source was defence solicitors, but their contributions were more variable. When there was a SER the solicitor often relied on it for background information and concentrated on describing current circumstances, but in many cases where there was no SER the solicitor did not offer detailed information on employment. The presence of a solicitor depended on several factors, including the defendant's view of the case and familiarity with the system, which might lead him or her to seek representation, and the court's policy in deciding legal aid applications. Though all courts worked on the principle of granting legal aid in serious cases, their practices varied somewhat; H1 in particular had a reputation for liberality. Defendants who had no one else to speak for them tended, in most cases, to give a bare minimum of information, even with patient questioning by the court.

At the L and LH courts these three – the SER, the defence solicitor or the defendant – were the usual sources of information. Occasionally there were others, such as an employer, doctor, or the prosecutor. But at the H courts an additional source, no longer used elsewhere, was the police statement of 'antecedents', which usually included brief social details on the offender. Though occasionally inaccurate or out of date, the antecedents were often useful, providing on average more information than was given by unrepresented defendants speaking for themselves, and their availability may possibly have contributed to the H courts' less frequent use of SERs.

Thus the amount of employment information varied considerably. At one end of the scale the court would be told what jobs, if any, the offender had held in the past, for how long, and why they had finished, together with some details of present employment or prospects. At the other extreme the bench would hear only whether or not the offender was employed now. Current status was mentioned in almost every case, though in some, especially at the H courts, details were scanty; in a substantial minority of cases nothing was said about employment history. Along with information on actual work the court would normally be told about the offender's means: his or her wages or benefit payments, and financial commitments. The amount of information on means was more consistent than that on work, but still varied somewhat. In most cases housing, food and fuel costs, and hire purchase commitments were mentioned, but other items like travelling expenses for work or job hunting were seldom covered. Existing fine commitments might or might not be made known. In nearly every case information on employment was given to the bench before they decided sentence, though sometimes further details emerged afterwards when the amount of a fine had been fixed and payment terms were being negotiated. In 9 per cent of the observed cases means information was given only at this stage. In 2 per cent the bench received no information at all about the offender's employment or means.

The nature and extent of employment information were largely influenced by the type of case and people's expectations as to sentence. Where it was almost certain that there would be only a financial penalty information might be limited to the offender's current employment status and means, fuller details being more likely to emerge in serious cases. But it is clear from the foregoing that there were also more haphazard variations. Consequently cases were encountered where the information was less than the offender might have wished to present and less than the court might have been willing to consider, and it was only because the researchers were focusing on such matters that they were aware of the gaps. In particular, some fines were fixed in cases where information on means, and other relevant matters, was seriously inadequate, and this is further elaborated on pp. 52–3.

Presentation and uses

Employment information was sometimes presented to the court as
relevant to the circumstances of the offence. Occasionally it was
aggravating: theft from an employer, for instance, would be very
much frowned on by the bench. Much more commonly it was
suggested in mitigation that the offending was partly due to unemployment, or had occurred in connection with the offender's efforts
to work. Alternatively, a steady work history or current job would be
advanced as evidence of good character in a plea for mitigation of
sentence. One or two interviewees suggested that this argument
might backfire if the court took the view that a person lucky enough
to be in work ought to have known better than to break the law, and
that a prison sentence would release his job for someone more
deserving; but no signs of such thinking were observed in the
courtroom. In several observed cases, especially at the L and LH
courts, the chairman made remarks at sentence which acknowledged
regard for employment as evidence of good character: at L2, for
example, a man convicted of a serious assault was given a suspended
sentence with the words, 'We have been helped by your frank

Table 3.1 Mitigating arguments featuring employment, in 410 observed
cases

Argument	No. of cases in which used
Good past work record/present attitude to work/efforts to get work (any of these mentioned as evidence of defendant's character)	59
Defendant's job/job prospects would be jeopardized by	
disqualification from driving	35
severe sentence	24
Defendant's job/earnings have already suffered due to offence/anticipated conviction	11
Unemployment/dwindling business for defendant/defendant's family helped to cause offending through poverty/worry/boredom/drink/glue sniffing etc.	47
Offending occurred in connection with defendant's/family's efforts to work/find work/get work	18
Defendant is unemployed so cannot afford high fine/compensation	3
Miscellaneous	9

admission and your lack of previous record, and your work record is in your favour.' Interviewees frequently used the word 'stability' in discussing the importance of employment. A further type of mitigation plea stressed the harm that would be done to the offender's job, or job prospects, by a severe sentence or by disqualification from driving (though in many of the latter cases all parties knew that disqualification would be mandatory); a variant of this was the argument that the offender's employment had already suffered because of the court case, and that therefore justice would be served by a lenient sentence.

Mitigation pleas as such were put forward by defence solicitors, but some of the material in SERs, and some of what defendants themselves said, could also be interpreted as mitigation. Table 3.1 shows, for the total of 410 cases observed at sentence in all the six courts, how often employment information was presented (by anyone in the case) in ways which the researchers thought could be seen as mitigating. For a few people more than one of the listed kinds of argument was used, and of course in many cases mitigation included material on other topics as well as employment. At each court employment arguments were thought to be a part of mitigation in not less than 30 per cent of the observed cases (and 42 per cent of those where there was a defence solicitor or SER).

No great difference appeared between the courts in the frequencies of the various kinds of argument shown in Table 3.1. But at the LH courts, though their unemployment rates were comparable to those at the H courts, the number of unemployed offenders whose advocates stressed their hopes of work, or reasons why they could not find it, resembled the number at the L courts whose advocates spoke cheerfully of their work prospects. Table 3.2 shows the figures which, though small, suggest a clear pattern.

Table 3.2 Unemployed defendants who were legally represented or had SER: whether anything was said in court about work hopes or prospects

Court	L1	L2	H1	H2	LH1	LH2
No. of defendants (100%)	10	10	25	34	42	23
Work hopes or prospects mentioned:						
No.	7	8	6	7	28	19
%	70	80	24	21	67	83

Table 3.2 implies either that people at the LH courts still clung to some hope of finding a job, or at least that their advocates thought it

useful to present them to the court in that light; whereas at the H courts unemployment was simply accepted as a fact of life. This is consistent with the expectation that the courts' responses to unemployment would vary with their local circumstances.

Whether or not SER material contained mitigation, probation officers' recommendations for sentence were an important piece of information for the bench to take into account. A few SERs in the observed cases linked their recommendation for a particular sentence with a specific reference to the offender's employment circumstances. For example, in one case a fine was recommended for a young man earning good money in his first job, as a salutary way of reminding him of his adult responsibilities; in another, a listless youth of low intelligence and with no prospect of work was recommended for attendance at a day centre where he would learn social skills. But most SERs did not make such explicit links; employment matters were just part of the whole picture the probation officer was presenting to the court. However, analyses of the records samples showed that, after allowing for offending scores, there were hints of a definite pattern in SER recommendations. Financial penalties were recommended more often for employed than unemployed men at five courts (all but L1), and so were suspended sentences at L1 and LH2. For the unemployed probation was preferentially recommended at L1, H2, and LH1, and community service orders at H2 and LH2. These statistical relationships, though small, supported the hypotheses that SERs on unemployed offenders would recommend some disposals rather than others. The extent to which magistrates followed them is reported in the next section.

One way in which courts used employment information is obvious: it was relevant to the amount and terms of a fine. (Financial penalties are discussed in detail on pp. 48–53.) Other ways have been implied in the comments above on mitigation. In addition, courts sometimes took lack of employment as a pointer to the possible existence of other problems. As already mentioned, four courts tended to get SERs more often for the unemployed. This suggests that for this group of people they felt there might be other matters needing investigation; and they were often right. Among the cases observed over all the courts one-third of the employed offenders seemed to have some kind of personal or social problem, but almost twice as many unemployed did, apart from the actual lack of a job, and among women who were fully occupied as mothers and housewives the proportion was even higher, at 78 per cent.[2] Many of the unemployed and the young mothers had multiple problems. In each of the three groups the most common problems apparent were financial and family worries, followed by medical or psychiatric problems and, especially among the unemployed, alcohol abuse; accommodation problems and drug misuse were mentioned less often. The picture was much the same at each court separately, and it helps to explain the tendency for more unemployed than employed offenders to be put on probation. This, and the links between employment status and other kinds of sentences, are discussed later.

From these results it can be seen that the presentation of information about a person's employment had several dimensions. In most cases it was possible to discern a pattern in the way that these related to each other and were determined, in particular, by the seriousness of the offence and the possible sentence. However, this was not always so: the patterns were only partial and often there were gaps. Although the study was concerned primarily with information about offenders' employment, it is likely that much the same considerations apply to information on other subjects, and to the whole process by which information is brought to the attention of the court. The patience and courtesy with which the court listened to defendants and their advocates, and the careful attention given to information offered, were frequently impressive. But there were constraints, including the pressure of time in a busy courtroom and sometimes, perhaps, a reluctance to probe into personal circumstances out of respect for the defendant's privacy. Ways need to be explored for reducing the communication gap which often seemed to exist between the bench and an inarticulate, unrepresented defendant, and for increasing the use of modern methods of information processing in the service of the court.

There remains the question of whether the employment information put before magistrates actually had any discernible impact on their decisions. This was hard to assess in observed cases; employment matters were only part of the total picture offered to the bench, and the researchers did not discuss individual cases with magistrates. It was guessed, usually from bench remarks like the L2 one already quoted, that employment matters had influenced the type of sentence (as distinct from the amount or payment terms of a fine) in not more than 10 per cent of the total. Ways in which this could happen were explored generally in the interviews. But to disentangle employment from other factors one must turn to the statistical evidence from the records samples.

Employment status and sentencing patterns

As an introduction to this topic, Table 3.3 shows the various ways in which all the men in the records samples were sentenced. The order in which the sentences (excluding deferment) are shown can be regarded as a rough scale of severity, running from discharge (or compensation only) as the least severe to immediate custodial sentence and committal to the Crown Court for sentence (implying the expectation of a custodial sentence) as the most severe. It is a crude measure, taking no account of the subjective impact of a penalty (e.g. a heavy fine) and disregarding the fact that probation is an individualized disposal. But the order shown is commonly used as an indicator of the tariff. As was expected, fines were by far the commonest disposal. When analyses took into account the men's offending scores (thus allowing for the effect on sentence of offence characteristics and previous criminal record) it was seen that each court used variations of an underlying pattern, as follows. The great majority of men with low to average scores were fined, and a few received a conditional discharge or a compensation order only, or a probation order. As the offending score rose, penalties spread 'up tariff' until the few men with the highest scores were likely to receive a custodial sentence. The main variations of this pattern were that at low to average scores LH1 frequently used discharges or compensation orders instead of fines, H2 and LH2 often made attendance centre orders for men under 21, and LH2 used CSO more than the others. Table 3.3 shows the contrast in custody rates between L1, H1, and LH1 on the one hand and L2, H2, and LH2 on the other, which reflected the research design.

Table 3.3 Sentences imposed on male property offenders

Court No. of men (100%)	L1 553	L2 517	H1 664	H2 585	LH1 599	LH2 552
	%	%	%	%	%	%
Sentence deferred	2	4	1	1	1	1
Discharge, compensation order only	9	7	12	7	19	4
Fine	54	44	57	52	41	39
Probation	13	14	12	6	10	6
Attendance centre	1	–	1	6	1	7
CSO	9	7	9	8	12	18
Suspended imprisonment	5	7	1	6	5	4
Immediate custody (detention centre, youth custody, prison)	5	15	6	15	8	18
Committed to Crown Court for sentence	3	3	2	1	2	2

Statistical analyses[3] then compared sentences between men who were employed on the day of sentence and those who were unemployed (omitting the few others). At each court the unemployed had, on average, noticeably higher offending scores, indicating that they were more serious offenders than the employed: a fact of interest in itself. Because of this difference the offending score had to be taken into account in comparing sentences. It was found that usually the type of sentence was much more strongly related to the offending score than to employment status. Nevertheless the latter often made a small independent contribution to the probability of certain sentences. Table 3.4 shows the results for men aged 17–20.

Table 3.4 Young men aged 17–20: relationships between employment status and the probabilities of particular sentences, offending score being allowed for

Court	L1	L2	H1 H2	LH1 LH2
Total no. of cases	211	214	253 243	238 215
Discharge, compensation order only	–	–	EU	– –
Fine	E***	–	–E**	E*E
Probation	U*	–	–U**	–E**
Attendance centre	/	/	/–	/–
Community service order	–	–	–U*	– –
Custodial sentence or committal for sentence	U***	–	–E*	U*U**

Key: E employed more likely than unemployed to get that sentence
U unemployed more likely than employed to get that sentence
– no relationship at P ≤ 0.20
/ number of cases too small for analysis
* the number of stars is a rough guide to the relative strengths of the relationships, the strongest being marked ***

Deferment of sentence is not included because the numbers at each court were too small for analysis.

Table 3.4 shows that four courts, especially L1, tended to use fines for the employed rather than the unemployed, independently of their offending scores. At L1 and H2 the unemployed were more likely than the employed to be put on probation, and at L1, LH1, and LH2 they were more likely to get a custodial sentence. Five other cells of the table show other relationships. Table 3.5 shows the results for men aged 21 and over.

Table 3.5 shows a more consistent pattern than Table 3.4. All six courts used fines more for the employed than the unemployed. For the employed, four used discharge (or compensation only), four used probation, three used CSO, and two used immediate custody. When men receiving custodial sentences were examined as a separate group three courts, especially LH2, were inclined to suspend sentences imposed on the employed. The detailed analyses showed that the discharge, probation, CSO, and suspension of custody the figures for the empty cells in Table 3.5 in fact had small differences in the same directions as the statistically significant

Table 3.5   Men aged 21+: relationships between employment status and the probabilities of particular sentences, offending score being allowed for

Court	L1	L2	H1	H2	LH1	LH2
Total no. of cases	316	292	374	300	326	319
Discharge, compensation order only	U**	U***	–	U*	–	U**
Fine	E***	E***	E*	E*	E*	E***
Probation	U***	U*	–	–	U**	U**
Community service order	U	–	U	–	–	U**
Suspended imprisonment	–	–	/	E	–	E***
Immediate imprisonment or committal for sentence	–	U***	–	–	–	U***
Those given any custodial sentence or committed for sentence:						
Total no. of cases	50	87	26	63	64	67
Suspension of sentence	–	E	/	E*	–	E***

Key: E employed more likely than unemployed to get that sentence
  U unemployed more likely than employed to get that sentence
  – no relationship at P $\leq$ 0.20
  / number of cases too small for analysis

  * the number of stars is a rough guide to the relative strengths of the relationship, the strongest being marked ***

ones indicated.

Together Tables 3.4 and 3.5 suggest that, offering scores being allowed for, the employed were more likely to be fined or (for those over 21) to receive a suspended sentence, and the unemployed were more likely to receive a discharge (or compensation order only), probation, CSO, or immediate custody. The pattern is stronger and more consistent for the men over 21 than for the younger ones, and (taking both age groups together) L1, L2, and LH2 show it more strongly than H1, H2, and LH1. The finding that employment status was significantly related to sentencing, but much less strongly than the offending score, is consistent with statements made by many of the interviewees. Both sets of evidence bear out the hypothesis that courts would heed information on both factors but treat offending as the more important.[4]

It was noted on p. 39 that the courts varied in the extent to which they called for SERs, and the L and LH courts obtained them slightly more often for the unemployed. The proportion of cases in which the bench followed the probation officer's recommendation for sentence varied between 53 per cent and 73 per cent, being greater at the 'low custody' courts than the 'high custody' ones, but there was no significant evidence that the rate of agreement differed between employed and unemployed. In cases of disagreement the sentence was more often 'up tariff' than 'down' compared with the recommendation, which is not surprising because probation officers try to offer the bench a non-custodial option even when they know it is unlikely to be accepted; but there was little difference between employed and unemployed in the use of 'up tariff' sentences in disagreed cases. Taken together these results imply that the courts each had their own ways of deciding for which offenders SERs would be useful, and on how to respond to the reports they received; and that only at the first of these stages, and only for the L and LH courts, was employment status a factor in the decision.

As already mentioned (p. 43) SERs at some courts showed a tendency to recommend fines and suspended sentences for the employed, and probation and CSO for the unemployed. These distinctions formed a partial pattern which fitted in with that of Tables 3.4 and 3.5. There was no evidence from the study to say how much of the fit was due to courts following the SER recommendations, and how much to probation officers recommending what they thought the court would be likely to accept, but either way one can say that the tendencies to differential sentencing shown by the courts appeared to some extent to be supported, or encouraged, by the probation service.

Tables 3.4 and 3.5 suggest that for the unemployed there was a bifurcation of sentencing at the tariff level of the fine. Some of those not fined were dealt with by way of discharge (or compensation order only) while others received probation, CSO, or a custodial sentence. Softley (1978), studying offenders sentenced in 1974 when unemployment was much lower, found a similar result, though on this point his analysis did not take seriousness of offending into account. The present findings suggest that the six courts were following a pattern, but that the two with relatively low unemployment (L1 and L2) and the 'high custody' court with transitional unemployment (LH2) were holding onto it more strongly than the other three which, as unemployment became more general, were moving away from it. This again supports the hypothesis that courts' responses to unemployment would be conditioned by their own experiences and their sentencing traditions. To understand better what was happening it is necessary to look more closely at particular types of sentence.

Financial penalties

When asked how unemployment had affected their work, many magistrates and court clerks immediately spoke of financial penalties and of the dilemma faced by benches in imposing fines appropriate to the offence on people of low incomes. They had tried to solve it in various ways: by lessening the amount of the fine, by giving longer to pay, and by seeking alternative penalties for the unemployed.

Their adaptations were not uniform but, as hypothesized, varied with each court's local circumstances and tradition. A comparison of the sums of money imposed on the men in the records samples showed a pattern, with (on average) the highest amounts at the L courts, the lowest at the H courts, and those at the LH courts in between; and each 'high custody' court tended to impose larger fines than its 'low custody' partner. Benches' agreed 'thinking points' for fines varied: for example, the 'going rate' for shoplifting was £150 at L2, £100 at LH1, and more like £50 at the H courts. Within this framework the unemployed were, on the whole, required to pay less than the employed. But this distinction was not so apparent in motoring cases for which, except at the H courts, benches seemed reluctant to depart from the Magistrates' Association's standard list of suggested fines. Nor was it observed in cases of social security fraud where, in contrast to their police counterparts, the DHSS prosecutors seemed to have a policy of asking for compensation orders regardless of the offender's financial circumstances, and magistrates apparently felt bound to impose them. In the records samples (property crimes prosecuted by the police) each court made rather fewer compensation orders against unemployed men: overall, 45 per cent of cases, compared with 54 per cent for the employed. Only LH1 made much use of compensation orders unaccompanied by any other penalty.

Altogether the use of lower financial penalties for the unemployed was very uneven. Of course there were bound to be differences according to individual circumstances: some offenders without a job on the day of sentence none the less had the means to pay substantial sums, and interviewees were quick to point out that an unemployed youth living with parents who charged him minimal board, as many seemed to, had more spending money than a breadwinner supporting a family on a low wage. But at nearly every court the probation service felt that some offenders were being fined beyond their ability to pay, and all the courts' samples threw up cases of unemployed people being ordered to pay more than £400.

For some offenders, especially the unemployed, paying fines dragged on for years. Nearly everyone paid by instalments which, for the unemployed, were usually fixed at £3 a week or £6 a fortnight to fit in with social security benefits. Although courts tried to observe the principle (stated by the Court of Appeal in R. *v.* Knight, 1980) that fines should be capable of being paid within 12 months, in practice it often did not work out like that. On average the unemployed were given longer than others to pay: of the unemployed men in the records samples up to 20 per cent of those fined, and 24 per cent of those ordered to pay other moneys, were initially given more than a year, and a few were given more than two years. Analysis of their payment records showed that many took far longer than the period originally allotted, especially when their fines had been imposed on top of others still outstanding.

Courts H1 and H2 had consciously adapted their fining policies to the prevailing high levels of unemployment. The emphasis was on keeping fines small, and both courts appeared to have a rule of thumb that as a person on supplementary benefit could afford weekly payments of at most £3 a week, to keep within the 12 months rule the maximum fine should be £150, though in practice some were larger. Magistrates felt that if fines were kept low there was no need for the unemployed to be at greater risk of default (though they were: see below). Because of this policy the H courts used fines for more of their unemployed offenders than the other four courts, and were less inclined to look for alternative penalties. Hints of these differences appear in the pattern of Tables 3.4 and 3.5. The search for alternatives was especially apparent at LH2 where, as will be discussed later, the bench increasingly turned to CSOs.

Informants at all courts except L2 felt that unemployment had increased the work of fines administration, as more people paid their fines by small instalments spread over longer periods. Several thought that the unemployed were more likely to default. This was borne out by an analysis of payment records, which showed that at each of the six courts men who had been unemployed when fined were more likely to get behind in their payments, to be brought back to court for enforcement action, and (for a small minority) to end up in prison with the fine written off. Default was higher among the serious offenders, who in turn were more likely to be unemployed, but analyses which took these links into account (by means of the offending score) found an independent association between unemployment and default: the unemployed were about three times more likely than the employed to progress through the sequence of default, issuance of a committal warrant, and imprisonment. The link between default and unemployment appeared greater than that found by Softley (1978) among offenders fined in 1974.

Observations of fine enforcement sessions at three courts (L1, H2, and LH1) gave a picture of many defaulters as people in a state of chronic financial muddle and mismanagement, often misunderstanding the court's expectations and priorities. Probation officers and solicitors interviewed said that many unemployed owed debts other than fines, and for such offenders debt had become a way of life: a constant series of attempts to balance one pressing payment against another, sometimes exacerbated by delays in receiving benefits. Fines were regarded as simply another complication. Other offenders just deliberately avoided paying their fines for as long as they could. The picture of many defaulters as being people on low incomes, often unemployed and with other problems, is consistent with the findings of Softley (1983) and Millar (1984).

These findings for the six courts in the study offer a picture of how rising unemployment has affected the system of financial penalties, why the use of fines has declined, and how the administrative burden on the courts has grown. If, as the NACRO working party urged in 1981, the fine is to be safeguarded as the pre-eminent penalty in the repertoire of British courts, the problems must be overcome. This could be largely achieved by a combination of three measures: an explicit system of means-related fines, the provision to courts of better information on offenders whom they propose to fine, and the availability of closer supervision and advice for fine payers.

First, a proper system of means-related fines would separate the two elements of the imposition process: matching the penalty to the gravity of the offence, and taking due account of the offender's means. In such a scheme magistrates would be free to impose the level of fine they thought appropriate to the offence (subject as now to any statutory limits), and the fines would be expressed in units, not actual money. Then court staff, having obtained details of the offender's means, would translate the number of units into money terms according to disposable income, using a common formula. This type of system is used in several European countries, where the units are known as day-fines. Although some people at the six courts expressed caution about the idea, the H courts' practice of gearing fines to the supplementary benefit level, with a notional ceiling of £150, already embodied something like the day-fines principle, and with it the H courts felt able to go on using fines freely for the unemployed. A day-fines system would facilitate efforts now being made to reduce unreasonable inequalities in sentencing between magistrates' courts. The Magistrates' Association's standard list of suggested fines for traffic offences aimed to reduce the great disparities previously noticeable in different parts of the country for similar offences, and many courts now use it as a guideline. But interviewees at the H courts said they did not feel able to, because the list did not allow for their local conditions of a depressed economy. At the LH courts, which had comparable unemployment rates, some of the highest fines on the unemployed were in motoring cases. The Magistrates' Association has been working on guidelines for a much wider range of offences, and this is to be welcomed. For monetary penalties a day-fines system would be a substantial help, because the guidelines would then define the penalties simply in terms of units which would be equally appropriate for all courts.

Second, the provision of better information on prospective fine payers in many cases is crucial. It was observed that, in spite of the care courts generally took, some fines were being fixed with the bench knowing very little – in a very few cases, nothing – about the offender's means. Most such fines were small, but eight were observed of over £100. For means enquiries each court had its own procedure, which could vary somewhat between sessions and cases, and some defendants escaped the net. But there is a wider aspect also: the provision of information which would enable sentencers better to decide in the first place whether an offender is a 'good risk' for a fine. This involves judging his or her attitude and likely response to the experience of being fined, and, though more research is needed on this topic, one factor which would probably be predictive of the risk is whether previous financial penalties have been successfully paid. The researchers came across cases where in several successive prosecutions, sometimes at different courts and often involving motoring convictions interspersed with others, an offender had built up a backlog of fines which seemed most unlikely to be collected, and which would surely have influenced the bench against a further fine had they been aware of the situation. In one such case a man already owing over £1,300 was fined for the fourth time.

None of the six courts had an adequate system for telling the bench about a defendant's previous fines. L2 came nearest, with computerized records which enabled the clerk to inform the bench if an offender up for sentence was in arrears of fines to L2. The staff said this arrangement enabled them to chase up defaulters promptly, and that they were less likely to be fined again. But even this system did not tell the bench of people whose payments on outstanding fines were up to date, or who owed money at other courts, which in urban areas might be fairly common. Nor did it give any history of past fines which had eventually been settled. At the other five courts, though some had computers, there was less routine information on existing fines, in spite of the staff's efforts to check records and question defendants. A deputy clerk said, 'We do try, but it's all rather hit and miss.'

One step towards a solution (suggested by staff at L2) would be to have all fines collected and enforced by an offender's 'home' court. Along with this change, records should be available so that sentencers could receive a list of *all* previous convictions (including motoring offences and others like failing to pay a TV licence, which are not normally included with 'criminal' records), identifying the home courts for any financial penalties. With computers which could link sets of records and speed enquiries between courts, such a system could, in many cases, give sentencers considering a fresh fine much better information than they get now.

Third, the availability of closer supervision and, where necessary, financial counselling of fine payers, by court staff trained for the purpose, could help many to avoid getting into serious default. Most fine payers are not under the eye of the probation service, and money payment supervision orders seemed fairly rare at any of the six courts. If fines enforcement officers, with a combination of firmness and sympathy, focused on the supervision of people and their debts as well as the court accounts, more fine payers might well heed the advice the researchers frequently heard magistrates offer: 'If you get into difficulties don't just leave it, come back to the court.' Financial management might also be assisted in some cases by fine payers on social security being allowed to opt for deductions from benefit at source. Employed offenders are allowed a similar facility through an attachment of earnings order; the unemployed, at present, are denied this option.

This is not the place for an extended discussion of enforcement methods, on which there is now a wealth of knowledge and practical guidance from the studies by Casale and Hillsman (1986) and Chandler (1987). But the measures outlined here could go a long way to release courts from the pressure they feel to seek alternative penalties for the unemployed. Sentencers could then consider non-monetary penalties in their own right, and not because they fear that some unemployed people cannot afford fines.

Community service orders

At each of the six courts the majority of the men in the records sample who were ordered to do community service were unemployed. At the H and LH courts the proportion was over 80 per cent; at H2 it was 95 per cent. This is a very different situation from that envisaged in 1970 by the ACPS, who had imagined the typical offender sentenced to CS as a working person who would carry out the order in his or her spare time. Statistical analyses showed that most of the CS men in the study had fairly high offending scores, so that the courts were using CS mainly as a high tariff penalty; but there was also an independent tendency to use it more for the unemployed. As Tables 3.4 and 3.5 indicate, this occurred at four courts, especially LH2. Cases observed in the courts were generally consistent with this picture.

The courts' regard for CS as a constructive way of dealing with unemployed offenders emerged strongly from the interviews and observations. People felt that CSOs were particularly relevant for the unemployed since they could not afford heavy fines, but also that CS gave them something constructive to do and provided some of the discipline of work. Some interesting paradoxes appeared. For example, is CS a soft option for unemployed offenders, since it does not deprive them of leisure time in the same way as those who are in work? This view was held at L2, where indeed there had once been an attempt to restrict CSOs to employed offenders, though in the longer term rising unemployment had made that impracticable. Obversely there was some sympathy for the view that, especially in areas of high unemployment, CSOs were now in some respects inequitable, since they bore more heavily on those who had jobs, but unlike Jardine, Moore, and Pease (1983) in Northern Ireland the study found no evidence of any difference in length of CSO between employed and unemployed.

Cutting across the general approval of CS as a penalty for the unemployed was a lively controversy about its place in the tariff. On the one hand it was held that a CSO should be used only for offenders who would otherwise have been sentenced to custody; on the other, that a CSO was available in all cases where the offence was punishable by imprisonment. This debate produced some tensions, and each court had tried to solve the problem in its own way. At L2 the policy was to use CS only in lieu of a custodial sentence and without regard to employment status. At L1, H1 and H2 it was seen mainly as an alternative to custody, but was sometimes thought suitable in other cases, especially for young people, and for some unemployed instead of fines. At LH1 the official policy was that CS was a high tariff sentence, but many magistrates liked it, especially for young people, and every now and then some tried to extend it down the tariff, meeting resistance from the probation service who would remind the Bench of the agreed policy.

The pressure to use CSOs instead of fines, and the problems which arose in consequence, were brought into sharp focus at LH2. This court's policy was to use CS both down tariff and up, and it made more orders than any other court, using them for 21 per cent of the unemployed men in the records sample. The Chairman said:

> On more and more occasions a Bench, noting that an offender is unemployed, will turn their minds to a CSO partly because of that. They see a CSO as a constructive use of the offender's time, but also as a method appropriate because his financial means are limited. Whether this is the right way to consider CS is a

different matter, but it's happening as a result of the court being increasingly pressurised by unemployment.

One question arising is how to deal with a breach of a CSO. Where an order is clearly designated as an alternative to custody, then the expectation is that a breach will be visited by a custodial sentence. However this could not be contemplated where CS is used instead of a financial penalty. Recognizing this difficulty, LH2 had a system whereby a CSO intended in lieu of custody was announced as such in the courtroom, and the court records were noted accordingly to guide a future bench in dealing with a breach. But a second danger with using CS in place of fines is that a subsequent conviction may result in a custodial sentence because the CSO, now on the offender's record, becomes regarded as the last step before prison. The list of previous convictions produced in court as information for a sentencing bench comes from the police, not the court records, and at LH2 there was no system for notifying the police of distinctions between CSOs. One way of meeting these points would be to have a recognized and officially sanctioned two-tier CSO. It would be agreed that if an offender had been given an order of, say, more than 60 hours then this was given in place of a custodial sentence, whereas below this level the order was being given as a non-custodial sentence in its own right. But at LH2, though some orders were short, the average order was 152 hours, and the observed cases did not always distinguish in length between high-tariff orders and others.

At courts with high unemployment there is likely to be some pressure on the CS places available. The LH courts were particularly interesting in this regard as they had responded to the problem in different ways. LH1, the second biggest user of CS among the six courts, deliberately kept orders short (their average length, 122 hours, was the lowest of the six) and tried to ensure that they were completed swiftly and in any case within a year. This enabled the probation service to organise a fast 'throughput' and meet all the demands of the bench under the official 'high tariff' policy. At LH2, on the other hand, magistrates were less inclined to modify the length of orders, despite efforts by the probation service to persuade them to do so. Consequently from time to time people who might have been eligible for CSOs did not receive them because there were no vacancies; and an analysis of such cases suggested that in this situation the unemployed were at increased risk of receiving an immediate custodial sentence instead.

In some respects the task of the probation service in organizing CS was easier with unemployed offenders, since activities for them could be scheduled during ordinary working hours, whereas the employed had to be catered for during evenings and weekends. Against this, however, it was said that employed offenders tended to be people who needed less direction, whereas many of the unemployed, especially those with no recent experience of work, required considerable supervision, and organizing work for them made greater demands on the service. At the H courts, where in effect the CS system had taken on the aura of an alternative work scheme for unemployed offenders, the organizers faced strong competition from other agencies for the 'community work' available. It was said that offenders were, as usual, at the end of the queue, and that projects for them were liable to be of poor quality. In the light of this experience of their colleagues in areas of chronically high unemployment, it was easy to understand the resistance in the LH1 probation service to extending the use of CSOs.

Such were the practical difficulties already encountered by courts in their efforts to operate the CS system in circumstances very different from those envisaged by its original planners. Were any arrangement whereby unemployed people had to work for their social security benefits to be introduced in this country, similar to the Workfare system that exists in the USA, the problems with CSOs would be compounded. Work without payment is what gives the CSO its retributive element. Under Workfare, work by an unemployed offender for a CSO might, in his or her eyes, become virtually indistinguishable from what he or she was obliged to do anyway in order to receive benefit.

Despite the various problems they experienced, many informants at all the six courts believed that, ideally, the CSO had great potential as a constructive sentence, and there was a strong wish to have it more freely available. A deputy chairman at LH2 probably spoke for many in saying that he would like to see the system expanded considerably, but that it was still in the pioneering stage with many anomalies which needed to be put right. A solicitor at L1 said, 'Until CS can be accepted as just another penalty, not tainted by its association with custody, its full usefulness will never be realised.' What then of the possibility of using it as an alternative to a fine? It is easy to see the appeal of this in places where unemployment is high. Indeed it might be argued that there would be something to be said in favour of an arrangement whereby offenders unable to afford financial penalties should work their sentence instead. But this raises a moral problem of creating class-based justice: offenders with money may pay for their transgressions, but those without are made to work.

Clearly there is an urgent need to consider, in these changed circumstances, what are the aims and purposes of the CSO. The preceding section of this chapter outlined ways of adapting the fines system so that financial penalties could be used equitably even for offenders on very low incomes. If this were done the CSO could be restored to its original place as a high-tariff alternative to imprisonment. But this is not what courts want. They see the CSO as a highly constructive measure which not only enables an offender to make positive reparation to society but which now also, in many cases, can meet his or her individual need, and in that respect it is like a probation order which is not tied to the tariff. It is thus essential to examine how the CS system should now develop, and to ensure that this happens in a just and equitable, rather than an *ad hoc*, manner.

Probation

A probation order is an individualized disposal, related to the needs of the offender rather than to the sentencing tariff. Interviewees at all courts said that if an unemployed offender received a probation order it would not be because of his or her unemployment *per se*, but because lack of work might be a pointer to other problems with which a probation officer could help (and which some employed people might also share). This statement, and the fact that at each court unemployed offenders seemed to have many more personal problems than employed ones (pp. 43–4) help to explain the different courts' tendencies to select the unemployed for probation (p. 47) and also for SERs (p. 39). In addition, perceptions by courts and probation officers of the role of probation were influenced by the local unemployment situation, by relationships between the service and the bench, and by the attitudes of both towards special employment schemes.

The six courts varied in their use of probation, from 6 per cent (of the men in the records samples) at H2 and LH2 to 14 per cent at L2. Four courts (the L and H courts) made probation orders more often for men under 21 than for older ones, which suggests that they regarded the younger men as being more likely to need supervision and guidance. But among the men over 21 the L and LH courts showed a tendency to use probation orders more often for the unemployed (Table 3.4). This was scarcely noticeable at the H courts (though H2, which made fewest orders anyway, showed it for the younger men). The pattern at the L and LH courts could be interpreted as suggesting that they were still inclined to see an adult man's lack of a job as something which might cause him problems needing a probation officer's support, whereas at the H courts unemployment and its associated troubles were an accepted fact of life which called less for special attention. The same possible explanation could be advanced for the parallel pattern of differences in the courts' use of SERs: the H courts did not share the propensity of the other four to use SERs more for the unemployed (though the availability of police antecedents may also have been relevant here).

At all the courts over half the men given probation were unemployed, and at the H courts and LH1 this proportion was three-quarters. No court distinguished in length of order between employed and unemployed. At no court was there a major expectation that probation officers should find jobs for their clients; it was agreed that the days when the probation officer could contact the friendly personnel manager of a local firm to place someone had gone. Instead officers concentrated on helping unemployed offenders to cope with other personal problems, to 'sort themselves out'. As well as individual counselling, and referring people to hostels and specialists when appropriate, probation officers ran groups for improving budgeting and social skills, for tackling alcohol and drug abuse, and for confronting offending behaviour. They were also the courts' main link with the Community Programme and the Youth Training Scheme. Magistrates generally favoured these schemes, viewing a place on one as equivalent to a job or at least the next best thing, but they mostly relied on the probation service to keep them informed of local ones and to take the initiative in finding places for individuals.

There were differences between the courts in expectations of what probation might achieve, in probation officers' own views of their work, and in their involvement with schemes. The L courts, when making a probation order, explained its conditions to the defendant in words which usually included a reference to employment. Interviewees said that, while probation officers were not expected to find people jobs, the court hoped that probation help might motivate unemployed offenders to find their own. This was apparent from remarks made by the chairman when announcing an order: e.g. at L1, 'You need supervision ... We're anxious that you should get into useful employment and settle down.' Probation officers at L1 agreed that most offenders could find work if they wanted, while the service at L2 ran a support group for job seekers. At neither court did probation officers have much contact with CP or YTS, though they occasionally pointed clients towards schemes.

Officers at the LH courts remembered the days when they had frequent and optimistic contact with local employers, but there were now few expectations that probation help would lead to a real job, though at LH2 officers were closely involved with several NACRO schemes, which they regarded as valuable for young single people (though not for others). At LH1 the service had little contact with schemes apart from a NACRO YTS, and they seemed to have taken a conscious decision that they could do very little about a person's job problems. At both courts officers concentrated on training offenders in life skills and personal development, and in making constructive use of leisure; if a client got a job this was seen as a bonus.

At the H courts the probation service was having an uphill struggle. Although officers now had to do less evening work, in almost all other respects unemployment made their tasks harder. They spoke of the low motivation and apathy of many of their clients who had been out of work for years, of the 'poverty of experience' of those who had never had a job, and of the prevalence of debt and other problems amongst families. Officers at H2 described parts of the town with very high rates of both unemployment and delinquency. They strove to persuade young people to use their time constructively at the various community facilities, and they themselves ran a day centre offering unemployed offenders a programme of social and practical skills. Magistrates thought well of this place, and in some cases made a probation order with a condition of attendance there instead of imposing a custodial sentence or a CSO. Officers at both courts encouraged clients to go on employment schemes, but they also said that some of the local ones did not offer worthwhile work or training, especially for offenders, who were often the last to be considered. NACRO schemes were not thus criticized, but for H2 the local NACRO one was too far away. At the time of the study the probation service at H2 was planning, together with the Apex Trust, a new CP scheme designed for offenders, and a year later was describing its progress in hopeful terms.

Magistrates generally respected and admired the work done by the probation service, though they sometimes tended to think of it as the traditional individual casework and did not always realize the other kinds of support it could offer. Magistrates also favoured work schemes, believing that they at least provided an orderly structure to the day and occupation for idle hands. But probation officers wanted to offer offenders something which they would experience as worthwhile in itself, especially where there was little hope of 'proper jobs'. In the areas of high unemployment they concentrated on helping their clients to live with unemployment and its consequences without getting into further trouble.

Walton (1987) writes of the dilemma facing the probation service: whether to try to address offenders' employment needs, by helping them acquire work-related skills and supporting them in job hunting; or to cater for their unemployment needs, by helping them adapt to life without work and find personal fulfilment in other legitimate forms of satisfying 'occupation'. Both responses were clearly seen in this study: the first at the L courts, the second at the H courts, while at the LH courts the dilemma seemed acutely felt. Overall, officers' attitudes towards dealing with their clients' workless state were ambivalent. Certainly they did not think work should be ignored, but there was also a strong feeling that it was not for the probation service to solve the problems of unemployment. They were sometimes sceptical about the value of special schemes, which were not financially worthwhile for family breadwinners and which, lasting only a year, could raise people's hopes and then dash them. But some officers felt the service could do more towards schemes especially geared to working with offenders. Employment and training schemes for offenders are discussed in later chapters, but the indications from this study suggest that more could be done to inform courts about schemes for the unemployed, and that there is a case for closer liaison between the courts, the probation service, and the providers of schemes. For this to happen the probation services, who play the key role, need to review their policy towards such provision.

This section has dealt with the work of the probation service for those offenders who were given probation orders, but of course they had many others under their supervision, especially people released from penal institutions to whom they gave similar care and whose unemployment problems were, if anything, worse. The service was also responsible for running the system of CSOs, whose anomalies and difficulties have been described. Officers may have been uncertain about their proper role in regard to their clients' job prospects, but from this study it is clear that, in the struggle to contain the problems which mass unemployment was causing for people involved in the criminal justice system, the probation service had a front line role.

Custody rates and sentencing shifts

The first section of Chapter 2 described the links between criminal justice and the traditional work ethic, interest in which was among the origins of this study: the idea that, for an offender facing sentence, a job and a steady work record were assets which could be put into the scales to weigh against anti-social behaviour. Thus (other things being equal) the employed would be less likely than the unemployed to be sent to prison. One aim of the study was to see whether this distinction still obtained, or whether courts had modified it in the face of widespread and increasing unemployment.

Modification might occur in more than one way. A court could continue sentencing the employed as usual but, recognizing that it was now less reasonable to expect the unemployed to find work – or even that sometimes the lack of work might have contributed to offending – it could become more tender to the unemployed, sending fewer to custody than before and thus reducing the sentencing differential. Alternatively a court could become more lenient towards its diminishing number of employed offenders, trying to protect their jobs, while sentencing the unemployed as usual; here the sentencing differential would grow. It would also grow at a 'tough' court which, in accordance with the hypothesis of Box and Hale (1982), began to increase its use of custody amid the 'rising tide' of unemployed. In any of these scenarios the change in the court's total custody rate, other things being equal, would depend on the proportions of employed and unemployed among the offenders whom it sentenced. In the second and third cases the custody rate would rise.

The various possibilities would have best been explored by comparing the sentences on large samples of employed and unemployed, for a number of courts, at several points in time. Because research resources did not allow this approach the cross-sectional design was used instead, pairs of courts being taken as examples of 'tender' and 'tough' ones operating in conditions of (relatively) low, transitional, and high unemployment. It was hypothesized that each of the six would use custodial sentences more for unemployed offenders than employed ones; that the differential would be greatest at the L courts, least at the H courts, and in between at the LH courts; and that it would be greater at the 'high custody' courts than at the 'low' ones. It is now time to look at the evidence.

Interviewees at all six courts, though least often at H2, said that in some marginal cases employment might save an offender from an immediate custodial sentence. They said that in contemplating custody the bench weighed all aspects of the matter, looking first at the nature of the offence and the offender's criminal record, and then at other things including family obligations; and that in a borderline case work was a 'plus factor' which might tip the balance. The clerk at L2 put it thus:

> I think one could draw a distinction by saying that someone with a good work record might be less likely to pick up a deserved prison sentence than someone with a bad record, on the grounds that there is a certain amount of unemployment and one wouldn't wish to increase that. But there is a distinction there between sending someone to prison because he's unemployed

61

and keeping someone out of prison because he happens to have a
job.

In adopting this view he, and his colleagues at the other courts, were
reflecting the approach put forward elsewhere: 'A sound record of
work and the undesirability of putting a high risk offender out of
work are good and obvious reasons for avoiding a prison sentence'
(*Justice of the Peace* 1982a: 684). The employed person might avoid
immediate custody either by a prison sentence being suspended, or
by the use of some different sentence. Examples were observed at
most of the courts, and statistical evidence from the records' analyses
(Tables 3.4 and 3.5) was broadly consistent with this picture.

But there were also differences in emphasis between the courts. At
L1 some respondents spoke of consideration for family breadwinners
and for offenders who, after long unemployment, had just found
work. Tables 3.4 and 3.5 suggest that custodial sentences were more
likely for the unemployed among men under 21, but not in the older
age group. At L2 there was more stress on a regular work record,
rather than just having a job on the day, and perhaps something of
the old traditional attitude appeared in the remark of the chairman
already quoted on p. 35. Tables 3.4 and 3.5 show a custody differential for the older men but not the younger, including a tendency for
prison sentences on employed men to be suspended. But there were
also suggestions at L2 that the court was more sympathetic to the
unemployed than formerly, so it may be that the differential had
decreased.

The H courts were an interesting contrast. H1, which had a general
reputation for leniency, made very few custodial sentences anyway,
and the tables show no difference in custody rates with employment
status. Interviewees, however, said that the bench would go to great
lengths to protect offenders' rare jobs, and several regretted that
suspended sentences were no longer available for people under 21.
Policy at H2, according to magistrates and clerks, was that employment status made no difference to the likelihood of custody, though
other informants said that sometimes it just might. The tables show
a tendency for prison sentences on employed men over 21 to be
suspended, while with the younger men slightly more of the
employed received custody – an anomalous result.

At LH1 interviewees did not speak much of employment status in
connection with custody, though it was agreed that a prison sentence
might be suspended for some employed. The tables show a slight
custody differential among the younger men. LH2 was perhaps the
most interesting court of all. The tables show a differential in both
age groups, and the tendency to suspend prison sentences on the

employed over 21 was much stronger than at other courts. This could imply the presence, as hypothesized, of the traditional work ethic. But a somewhat different interpretation could be put on the following words of the chairman:

> The Bench may feel that, on balance, the person perhaps ought to go to custody, but then maybe he's a young man just getting settled into a job opportunity, apparently making a go of it, and a custodial sentence will result in losing it. *This issue is likely to weigh more with the Bench nowadays than it would have done some years ago.* (emphasis added)

This suggests that at this relatively 'tough' court the custody differential now owed something to an increased tenderness towards the employed; and in addition a solicitor said that the court's attitude to the unemployed was changing. However, in all this it should be noted that the statistical samples were mainly of men sentenced in 1984, while the interviews took place up to 18 months later. The time lag might be expected to affect the findings most at the LH courts which were most subject to, and conscious of, the changes in unemployment.

Altogether the evidence went some way to support the hypothesis that courts would use custody more for the unemployed; and, in so far as the differential was greatest at the L courts and LH2, it bore out the hypothesis that the effect would vary with sentencing traditions and with experiences of unemployment. But, as is shown below, the differential was actually very slight. Moreover no court showed any significant difference between employed and unemployed in the lengths of immediate custodial sentences imposed. With suspended sentences H2 on average used shorter tems for unemployed men than employed ones, but suspended them for slightly longer; the other courts showed no differences.

Tables 3.4 and 3.5 together imply that for the unemployed there was overall, a slight shift in sentencing stemming from two points on the tariff: the fine and the suspended sentence. (All the courts in fact had some inclination to suspend prison sentences on the employed.) The pattern is more marked at the L courts and LH2, but all show it to some extent. Since these six courts, which were deliberately chosen for their contrasts in sentencing practices and experiences of unemployment, exhibited this common tendency, it is reasonable to surmise that other magistrates' courts might do so too, and that in the absence of better evidence the six together could be used as an indicator of the national picture.

On this assumption an analysis of the total records sample produced estimates of the changes in sentencing that would be expected among all males over 17 sentenced for property offences by magistrates' courts (in England and Wales) if the national unemployment rate were to rise by one percentage point within the range 7 per cent to 15 per cent.[5] Applying the estimates to the total of approximately 209,000 such cases in 1984 (Home Office 1984a) resulted in Table 3.6.[6]

Table 3.6 Estimates of sentencing changes among 209,000 male property offenders following a 1 percentage point rise in the national unemployment rate

44	fewer will have sentence deferred
320	more will be discharged or ordered to pay compensation only
677	fewer will be fined
163	more will be put on probation
50	more will be sent to an attendance centre
150	more will receive a community service order
132	fewer will receive a suspended prison sentence
163	more will be sent immediately to custody (or committed for sentence)

Thus, among other changes, approximately 163 more men would go into custody. This number is 0.27 per cent of the approximately 61,400 males over 17 received into penal institutions under sentence in 1984 excluding fine defaulters (Home Office 1984b). The estimates cover only property offenders, but these are about 70 per cent of the indictable cases dealt with by magistrates, and there is no reason to suppose that changes for the other 30 per cent would be greater. It can be seen that the impact of unemployment on prison sentences, as estimated by this study, is far smaller than that estimated by Box and Hale and discussed in Chapter 2.

Various explanations could be suggested for the discrepancy. One is that the limitations of the records samples, and the statistical methods used for analysing them, may have led to links between employment and sentencing being under-estimated. But probably of more significance is the fact that, for the reasons mentioned on p. 28, the study was confined to magistrates' courts. Perhaps if Crown Courts, which make much more use of prison, were to be included a different picture would emerge, and clearly there is now a strong case for extending research to them.

There are further aspects of the matter, one being the possible existence of a 'ratchet' effect. The pattern in Tables 3.4 and 3.5 suggests that for some of the unemployed who were not fined there was a tendency for sentences to be displaced up tariff. This effect could accumulate over subsequent prosecutions; for example, if a CSO is used instead of a fine then, as things stand at present, the next time the same offender appears for sentence the chances of a custodial sentence are likely to be increased. Thus unemployment would accelerate an offender's movement up tariff as his or her record of convictions lengthens. This possibility could not be explored by the analyses of Tables 3.4 and 3.5, but some slight evidence for it among the 17–20 year olds was offered by the fact that in this age group (though not in the older one) the propensity of the unemployed to have higher offending scores than the employed was greater at each 'high custody' court than at its 'low custody' partner. One factor in the offending score was the severity of previous sentences, which for many young offenders would have been imposed by the same court, so that a more severe approach would increase the chance of it being repeated on the next occasion.

Second, there is the possibility that unemployed offenders more often commit the kinds of crime which attract imprisonment. Although the study did not set out to explore links between unemployment and crime the issue could not be avoided. Several interviewees, particularly in the areas of high unemployment, volunteered the opinion that unemployment was a factor in the increases in certain crimes in recent years. This view gained some support from the statistical evidence: in the records samples the proportion of burglary cases was highest at the H and LH courts. Added to this is the fact that at each court the unemployed had higher offending scores. These considerations hint at a complex cyclic relationship between crime and sentencing in which unemployment plays one of the key parts.

This overview of sentencing has said little about some decisions. Deferment of sentence and the use of attendance centres (for men under 21) bore little relationship with employment status, though Table 3.6 includes them in the total picture. Deferment was rare at all courts except L2,[7] and only H2 and LH2 made much use of attendance centres (though the clerk at L2 wished that one were available there). Disqualification from driving, which cannot be used as a penalty on its own, was often feared by the employed (see Table 3.1) but in many cases magistrates had no discretion. The fact that employment matters had little bearing on bail has already been mentioned (p. 38).

Chapter 2 (p. 28) described the general hypothesis of the study and summarized the series of specific hypotheses which were derived concerning the importance of employment information to courts, disparities in sentences and other decisions as between employed and unemployed, and variations in these disparities between the six courts. Altogether there were 21 of these hypotheses, of which 14 were sustained in whole or in part. Appendix 1 in Crow and Simon (1987) itemizes the results; this chapter has presented the main ones in the context of the research design and of the issues discussed in Chapter 2. On the broad view, it is clear that unemployment has had a considerable impact on the administration of justice at magistrates' courts. Its effect on the numerical distribution of sentences has been small, though even a slight increase in imprisonment is something that should command attention. But the impact on financial penalties and their enforcement, on probation, and on the system of CSOs has been substantial and has caused many difficulties which have yet to be resolved. Unemployment also affected the ethos of the courts studied. As some interviewees commented, the magistrates' court is a local institution: it is part of the local community and is affected by what is happening in it. Certainly in the high unemployment areas there was an acute awareness of the problem. Magistrates, court staff, probation officers, and solicitors were concerned for the long-term unemployed, for families in debt, and for young people growing up without work.

Some courts still showed evidence of the traditional work ethic, but there was little to suggest that magistrates were overtly punitive towards the unemployed; rather, many were extra wary of doing anything that might jeopardize the jobs of those in work. Thus this research offers scant support for the radical view that courts are using their powers of punishment to contain a social threat posed by the swelling ranks of the unemployed. Instead, the predominant effect is to support the alternative explanation: that unemployment operates to restrict people's options. Magistrates said frankly that they felt constrained in their choice of appropriate methods to deal with offenders and, as has been seen, their search for ways out of the dilemmas led to anomalies and problems. Probation officers were hampered in their work, as unemployment sapped their clients' motivation to change and the service competed with other community agencies for opportunities which could give offenders constructive activity. The results of the study imply that the courts, probation services, and the Home Office need to develop policies to take account of the impact of unemployment, without prejudice to their fundamental tasks: otherwise unemployment will affect them and the offenders with whom they deal in ways over which they have no planned control.

Unemployment restricted offenders' options too. Many could no longer offer a good work record or the firm prospect of a job in mitigation of sentence. Paying fines was a struggle. Some were handicapped even before their case was decided: a solicitor at LH2 said that his unemployed clients often failed to give him proper instructions and came late to court, and that lack of work seemed to affect their whole attitude to dealing with life. Young offenders who had never worked, and older ones who felt they would never work again, lived with shrinking horizons. Several interviewees spoke of the need to find other ways than paid employment by which people could gain worth, self-esteem and social acceptance. Such a development would be welcome, but would require changes in social attitudes which may take some time to happen. Meanwhile unemployed offenders, having been dealt with by the courts, return to the community (sooner or later) still facing the prospect of a life without work. It is this context that gives significance to the subject of the next chapters: the provision for offenders of employment and training schemes.

Notes

1 A few interviewees said they felt that, although dealing with the offence had always been the primary concern of the bench, this had come to the fore even more in recent years and social information, such as that relating to employment, was perhaps less important than it used to be. Such remarks could imply that rising unemployment led to a matter-of-fact acceptance of defendants' workless state, as at the H courts. Alternatively they would be consistent with a general shift in emphasis from 'treatment' to 'just deserts' as suggested on p. 27. However, they were not made at every court, and other evidence suggested that some benches were paying more rather than less heed to employment matters – see, for instance, the remark of the LH2 chairman quoted on p. 63.
2 Analyses showed that the higher incidence of apparent problems among the unemployed could not be accounted for by their being more often the subject of SERs which brought problems to light.
3 Tables 3.4 and 3.5 were derived from multiple linear regression analyses which attempted to predict, for each type of sentence in turn, the probability of an offender receiving that sentence (as against all others), taking into account first the offending score and then employment status as independent variables. Though the data did not meet all the statistical assumptions required by multiple linear regression, further analyses using a multinomial logit model (Fry and Gill, unpublished) confirmed the general pattern of results. For further explanation see Crow and Simon (1987).
4 Even both factors together left the major part of the variation unaccounted for in the regression analyses. This is probably explained partly by the statistical limitations of the method and partly by the restricted amount of information contained in the two measures. Apart from the division into two age groups, factors other than offending score and employment status on the day of sentence were not included in these statistical analyses of sentencing patterns. None the less the overall picture given by the analyses is consistent with evidence from the rest of the study.
5 The upper limit of 15 per cent reflects the 'ceiling' implied by the fact that at that point the LH courts had the same proportion of

unemployed among their offenders as did the H courts though for the latter unemployment in the local population had risen to over 20 per cent. Using the samples from all courts together allowed for the fact that the H courts made less distinction in sentencing with regard to employment status.

6   A rise of one percentage point in the national unemployment rate would mean that (a) in the general population approximately 230,000 more people would become unemployed, and (b) in the population of 209,000 male property offenders over 17 sentenced by magistrates' courts approximately 6,270 more men would become unemployed. For every 1,000 of this latter increase, 26 more of the total sentenced would go to prison. Appendix 4 in Crow and Simon (1987) shows the calculations.

7   Discussing deferment, interviewees at all the courts said that the bench might defer sentence if there were real prospects of substantial and specific improvements in a defendant's circumstances, which might include a job; but all agreed that deferment was seldom used nowadays. The chairman at LH1 said it had not worked out as well as had been hoped when it was introduced, and that many people re-offended during the deferment period.

Chapter four

Employment and training schemes, and offenders

During the late 1970s and early 1980s the level of unemployment in the UK rose dramatically. A number of factors contributed to the rise in unemployment. These have been documented at length elsewhere, but they included the 'baby boom' of the 1960s which resulted in an increase in the number of young people entering the labour market (Showler and Sinfield 1981) and major shifts in Britain's economic structure, away from manufacturing and towards financial and other services. Levels of unemployment varied throughout the country, however, and the long term unemployed in particular tended to become concentrated in areas where labour-intensive, heavy manufacturing industry was in decline. The West Midlands, for example, which had been a centre for engineering industry, saw a deterioration from 5.5 per cent unemployed in 1977 to 15.5 per cent by 1985.

In addition, inner city areas contained a high percentage of people out of work. West and Martin (1979) reported that this reflected the higher proportions of semi-skilled and unskilled people living in the inner cities. These areas highlighted the general decline in local employment opportunities and a '20–30 per cent fall in manufacturing in most inner cities between 1971 and 1976'. The labour force survey of 1985 demonstrated that those in unskilled occupations were more likely to experience unemployment (Table 4.1). Inequalities in the distribution of unemployment also exist for different age groups, for different races, and for the ill and disabled (Showler and Sinfield 1981).

Programmes for the unemployed

Programmes of one kind or another, for the unemployed and those at risk of periods of unemployment, have been in existence in the UK and other western industrialized countries for some years now. The forerunners of current provision in this country can be traced to

69

Table 4.1 Social class and unemployment (GB)

	% of labour force	% unempl.	% of social class unempl.
Professional, intermediate & skilled	72	37	5
Partly skilled occupations	16	15	10
Unskilled occupations	6	7	13
Not occupied	5	41	81
TOTAL	(26,553,000)	(2,814,000)	

Source: Department of Employment (1986) *Labour Force Survey, 1985.*
Note: Percentage unemployed overall is 11%.

schemes developed in the United States in the 1960s as part of the War on Poverty programme. UK provision has also been modelled on the Canadian Local Initiative Programme (LIP) introduced in 1971, and it was this that informed the thinking behind the early UK programmes run by the Manpower Services Commission. The MSC's programmes have subsequently evolved through a succession of schemes, covering not only provision for the unemployed (such as the Job Creation Scheme, the Special Temporary Employment Programme, the Youth Opportunities Programme, and the Community Enterprise Programme) but various subsidies and training courses designed to keep people in jobs or equip them for future ones (e.g. the Temporary Employment Scheme, the Training Opportunities Programme, and the Technical and Vocational Education Initiative). This chapter and the next are principally concerned with two of the more recent employment and training programmes, the Youth Training Scheme (YTS) and the Community Programme (CP), and in particular with the way that an agency concerned with offenders, NACRO, has operated them. But it is important to see these schemes in relation both to the programmes that preceded them and to the wider employment and economic policy of recent years.

Studies of earlier schemes show that the assumptions underlying them, and consequently the aims they set out to achieve, were often poorly defined (Marshall, Fairhead, Murphy, and Iles 1978). Of the War on Poverty programmes, Marris and Rein (1974: 61) say: 'the constant interaction of means and ends makes the goals and assumptions of the projects hard to define'. Even so, it is clear that such objectives as can be identified have changed considerably over the years, both in this country and abroad, and between one form of provision and another. This is partly because the lessons learned from previous programmes have been transferred to subsequent ones. But more important have been changes in the economic climate, which have radically altered the nature of employment schemes. The schemes of the 1960s and early 1970s tended to take the form of 'special measures', which were special in two respects. First, they were directed towards people and areas with special needs, usually characterized as being deprived and disadvantaged. Second, they were special because full employment was the norm. Schemes were therefore seen as short-term measures to cope with cyclical unemployment and to ease people through a period of transition (viz. 'Special Temporary Employment Programme'). The schemes were generally regarded as interim measures; staging-posts on the way back to the normality of full-time, long-term jobs. But in the 1980s this changed. Unemployment became high, sustained and structural, and as it did so it engulfed a greater range of people and areas. The programmes that developed therefore became larger in scale, and general rather than special in nature, involving a wider section of the population. Another development of the 1980s has been for employment and training schemes to become more closely entwined with the government's labour market strategy and economic policy. This means that they can no longer be judged purely on their own terms but have to be seen as an aspect of policy.

The main, new strategy introduced at the beginning of the 1980s was the New Training Initiative (NTI) (MSC 1981a). This put the emphasis on producing a better trained workforce, able to respond to the needs of industry and commerce. It was first launched in a consultative document from the Manpower Services Commission in May 1981 and its development was subsequently set out in various MSC and government documents during the first half of the decade. The MSC's consultative document was followed in December 1981 by *An Agenda for Action* (MSC 1981b) and, at around the same time, by a government White Paper, *A Programme for Action* (Department of Employment 1981). In January, 1984 a further White Paper, *Training for Jobs* (Department of Employment 1984), restated the original objectives and went on to review progress up to then and to outline the next steps proposed by the government. It stated that 'training must ... be firmly work-orientated and lead to jobs'. It also endorsed the MSC's adult training strategy as 'in line with the market oriented approach to training'.

The New Training Initiative had three main components. The objective of the first was to develop occupational skill training to enable young people to acquire recognized standards of skills appropriate to the jobs available. It was not directly related to the kind of schemes with which this and following chapters are concerned, but an MSC document on this strand of the NTI, *Modernisation of Occupational Training* (MSC 1984b) did indicate that there were links with other aspects of the NTI, including YTS and the development of adult training. The second component of the NTI was concerned with preparing school-leavers for work and training. Its objective was to ensure that all those under 18 had the opportunity of continuing in full-time education, or entering training or a period of planned work experience combining work-related training and education. The Technical and Vocational Education Initiative was one measure intended to assist the transition from school to work. Another was the Youth Training Scheme. The third component of the NTI concerned adult training. It aimed to open up widespread opportunities for adults, whether employed, unemployed, or returning to work, to acquire, increase or update their skills and knowledge. This element of the NTI was the subject of an MSC discussion paper, *Towards an Adult Training Strategy* (MSC 1983a). This stated that, 'the main and most immediate emphasis of an adult training strategy should be economic' (para. 17). More effort, it was argued, should be put into training or retraining those already in or starting in employment than into speculative training or training for stock. Providing a skills base for a flourishing economy would be the most practical way of opening up opportunities for the unemployed. A later part of the paper referred to providing opportunities for unemployed people who were unable to benefit from occupational training. The need here, it was believed, was for basic education and training, and in this context it was suggested that there was scope for 'building up training openings in the Community Programme'. In a section on adult training, the White Paper *Training for Jobs* (Department of Employment 1984: para 40 (b)) also referred to the role that the MSC might play in helping the unemployed,

> who need training at a more basic level to restore their chances
> of getting a job after long periods of unemployment.... Such
> training might be provided through the short work preparation
> courses already provided under the Commission's Training
> Opportunities Programme, or in conjunction with the existing
> Community and Voluntary Projects Programmes.

Although there were a number of programmes in operation during the 1980s, the main ones were the Youth Training Scheme for young people leaving school and the Community Programme for long term unemployed adults.

The Youth Training Scheme

The Youth Training Scheme was intended to form part of the second component of the NTI, preparing school-leavers for work and training. It succeeded the Youth Opportunities Programme. Giving effect to the second element of NTI was one of the aims of the *Youth Task Group Report* (MSC 1982) which set out the arrangements for YTS. In the report it was made clear that the scheme was intended to be about 'providing a permanent bridge between school and work. It is not about youth unemployment' (para. 1.1). The specific aims of the scheme were to be:

a) To provide a better start in working life through an integrated programme of training, education and work experience ... which can serve as a foundation for subsequent employment, training and education ...;

b) To provide for the employer a better equipped young workforce which has acquired some competence and practical experience in a range of related jobs or skills ...;

c) To develop and maintain a more versatile, adaptive, motivated and productive workforce. (para. 4.3)

These remained the central objectives of YTS, but in the spring of 1985 the Government announced proposals to develop both the TVEI and YTS further, making YTS a two-year scheme. The White Paper *Education and Training for Young People* (Department of Education and Science and Others 1985) sought to link school and work preparation more closely, saying: 'The objective is clear: to produce by age 18 a very much larger flow than at present of qualified young workers capable of meeting the skill requirements of a modern economy either directly or after some further training' (para. 24). The new, extended YTS 'will differ from the existing YTS in that its objective will be that all trainees should have the opportunity to seek recognised vocational qualifications' (para. 30). Attention was also to be given to better ways of charting performance and achievement, and improving the structure of qualifications within YTS.

YTS started in April 1983 and became fully operational in September of that year. In the financial year 1983–4 the scheme cost £697.5m and had 397,200 entrants. In 1985–6, the last year of the old, one-year form of YTS, there were 389,400 entrants at a cost of £818.2m. An important feature of the old YTS was the existence of different modes. The main distinction was between Mode A, employer-based schemes, and Mode B, which included Community Projects, Training Workshops and Information Technology Centres

(ITECs), largely run by local authorities and non-statutory organizations. Once the intention to replace the original form of YTS by the two-year version, with its shift in favour of employer-led schemes, became apparent, there were progressive cut-backs in Mode B provision. Under YTS 2 Mode B provision was effectively replaced by 'premium places', a form of topping-up funding to certain managing agents to enable them to provide for certain groups with additional needs.

The Community Programme

The Community Programme was not intended to be a major part of the NTI. It was more in the nature of an old–style work programme for the unemployed although, as has been seen, some of the documents dealing with the development of NTI refer to its potential for contributing to the adult training component. The Community Programme succeeded the short-lived Community Enterprise Programme in 1982. The announcement in the Budget of that year that CP was to replace CEP caused much controversy at the time because CP was seen as inferior to CEP in both the money available for it and the reduced training element that would be included. The Community Programme was defined as a programme which

> provides full-time or part-time temporary jobs on projects which benefit the community. ... A period of work on a project under the Community Programme will enable people to acquire or re-acquire the habits and disciplines of work, to gain experience of the job they undertake on the project and, in many cases, to receive training. At the end of their period on the project they will also have a recent reference and this, together with the work experience and training should enhance their ability to compete for jobs. (MSC 1983b: para. 5.6)

This definition remained the basis of the CP subsequently, but there were several developments. One was an increase in the size of the programme from 150,000 to 255,000 places, announced in the 1985 Budget. Expenditure on CP increased from £400.1m in 1983–4 to £683.8m in 1985–6. Another development, following the publication of a report, *Value for Money in the CP* (Norrington, Brodie, and Munro 1986), was to place more emphasis on the quality and cost-effectiveness of CP schemes. There were also moves to enhance the training element within CP to enable it to contribute more to the adult training strategy; to mount national initiatives using CP in order to contribute to public policies on crime prevention, environmental improvement and energy conservation; to increase the involvement of business and commercial employers through company-led projects; and to encourage projects with the potential to create permanent jobs.

The fact that the Programme was different from the main training initiatives was underlined by it being referred to in documents under headings such as 'Help for Special Groups' rather than 'Training and Preparation for Work' (MSC 1983b), and 'Special Employment Measures' (MSC 1984a) rather than 'Occupational and Adult Training'. One point worth noting about both YTS and CP is that, although there were various expressions of hope that the programmes would help participants to compete for jobs, they were not intended to be job creation schemes. A government publication, *Employment: the Challenge for the Nation* (HMSO 1985), made it clear that the government was looking to other ways in which employment would be generated. The government's role in this respect was seen to be a limited one, a role based on encouraging the right climate. This it was doing by controlling inflation, by 'increasing the incentive to the unemployed to take jobs by further raising tax thresholds in real terms and reducing National Insurance contributions from the lower paid' (HMSO 1985: 23). 'Jobs', it was said, 'come from customers and nowhere else' and therefore the creation of jobs depended on the people of Britain showing enterprise and being willing to take risks (HMSO 1985: 3). The limitations of the two programmes, YTS and CP, in relation to job creation were also implicitly recognized by the development of other initiatives by the MSC more explicitly directed towards this goal, such as the Enterprise Allowance Scheme and the ENTRAIN initiative to promote new enterprise within YTS.

Schemes for unemployed offenders

Just as the evolution of schemes for the unemployed goes back over some years, so there is a history of schemes for unemployed offenders in particular. There is indeed some connection between the two since several of the early employment schemes in the USA were specifically linked to the crime problem and were located in high crime areas (Marris and Rein 1974). In this country several studies of offenders during the 1960s and 1970s commented on the lack of assistance for unemployed offenders. Martin (1962) found that few of the men in his sample had been assisted in obtaining employment by welfare workers. In a study of parolees, Morris and Beverley (1975) found that, of those who obtained work on their release, most did so through their own efforts, and none through the help of a probation officer. Silberman and Chapman (1971), in a study of two Probation

Service After-Care units, found that less than 15 per cent of their clients were given direct help with employment problems. Tidmarsh, Wood, and King (1972) commented on the need for more provision for homeless offenders in the form of sheltered employment and workshops.

Such assistance as there has been has tended to come either via the Probation Service or from specialist non-statutory agencies. Notwithstanding the findings reported above, in addition to their regular work with clients probation services have mounted special schemes (such as the Bulldog employment scheme), day centres with work-related activities, and during the 1970s several job development and placement services were established (Harding 1978: 23–6). One of the first and best-documented non-statutory schemes was the Apex Trust's Placement Service (Soothill 1974). Employment schemes have also been developed by the Burnbake Trust, the Peter Bedford Project and by NACRO. For the most part the schemes originally took the form of supported work projects. They tended to be special projects for a group with special employment problems. They also tended to be small in scale, unable to cater for more than a small minority of offenders.

However, as Chapter 2 has pointed out, for offenders and those working with them, unemployment has always been a problem, pre-dating the rise in unemployment nationally. This is partly because a criminal record has sometimes made it difficult for a person to get a job (Boshier and Johnson 1974) but also because people convicted of offences tend to come from sectors of the population who are most at risk of unemployment or are disadvantaged in the labour market because they have few qualifications. One consequence of this was that in the past schemes for unemployed offenders were seen as rehabilitative, in the sense that their aim was to compensate for these deficiencies and to re-integrate offenders (especially ex-prisoners) into what was taken to be normal working life. In other words the principal outcome looked for was that the participants should go on to regular, full-time employment. Another feature of such schemes was that the emphasis was very much on the individual offender, rather than the needs of the labour market. There was also some expectation, implicit if not explicit, that the schemes could reduce re-offending – about which, more shortly.

Originally much of the funding for employment schemes for offenders came either from Probation Committees, in the case of Probation Services, or from the Voluntary Services Unit of the Home Office in the case of the non-statutory sector. In recent years employment schemes for offenders have increasingly taken advantage of the funding available under the major MSC sponsored programmes: YTS, CP and VPP. This has had a considerable impact on both the individual schemes and the agencies, like NACRO, that have managed them. It has meant that the schemes have had to have regard, first and foremost, to the requirements of the programmes, and they have had to respond to a series of changes in the programmes and in the funding arrangements for them. It has also meant that the fortunes of the managing agencies have become very much tied to the development of such programmes.

Undoubtedly this alignment of schemes for offenders with general provision has had some benefits. It has placed employment and training, rather than the 'offender' label, at the forefront of concern. Although programmes may have undergone changes they have at least given the agencies operating them a decade or more of sustained, if variable, income with which to do the job. This is a considerable improvement on the preceding state of two or three years' money followed by an uncertain future. On the other hand it has been all too easy for the needs of special groups, such as offenders, to be overlooked or set on one side in programmes which are primarily geared to the needs of the economy in general, and industry and commerce in particular. Sustained lobbying by NACRO and others has been required to ensure that the needs of such groups are given due consideration. Also some ambiguities have arisen regarding the aims and objectives of such schemes. Are they principally about employment, training, and jobs, or are they about working with offenders? If, as some might argue, they ought to be about both, then the relationship between the two needs further consideration than it has so far received. It cannot be taken for granted that the availability of MSC funding for running schemes for offenders is without question a good thing. The case needs to be considered.

Criteria for success

As has already been noted, the objectives of employment schemes were sometimes ill-defined, but they included, in the past at least, some hope that those taking part in them would go on to full-time employment. With schemes for offenders there has often been the added expectation that they might lead to reduced offending. These aspirations have therefore tended to become adopted as the criteria for a successful scheme. Unfortunately only a few of the schemes for offenders have been the subject of adequate research. Of those that have been studied, most are in the USA and very few in the UK. Where such studies have been carried out the results have not been promising. Attempts to develop the employment potential of prisoners prior to release showed no improvement in terms of reduced reconviction rates (Davies 1974: 107). In the United States Taggart (1972), reviewing many attempts in the 1960s to improve employment and re-offending rates for offenders, concluded that this work:

> leaves little room for more than the most restrained optimism. There have been a wide range of projects to test the effectiveness of various strategies; and though the evidence which has been gathered is limited, very little of it is positive. There is no proof that any single manpower service or strategy has had more than a marginal impact on its recipients, and no proof that any combination of services can make a substantial contribution. On the basis of the existing evidence, it does not seem likely that the employment problems of offenders can be significantly alleviated by manpower programmes, or that these programmes will have a noticeable impact on the rate of crime. (cited in Davies 1974: 109)

The experience of undertakings such as Project Crossroads and the Rikers Island Project in the States was enough, Taggart contended, to counteract any 'inflated hope of success in increasing employability or reducing recidivism'. Such pessimistic conclusions are reinforced by experience in this country. A study of the Apex Trust's placement service showed that relatively few ex-prisoners were actually helped into employment for any significant length of time and,

> There is not really any indication that the Apex service has any definite effect in reducing the proportion of men who are reconvicted within one year after release. ... Even when one examines the reconviction rate of those who fully accepted the Apex service, there is no evidence that they have a significantly lower reconviction rate than any other group. (Soothill 1974: 119–20)

Interestingly, in subsequent analyses it was found that those who got jobs by their own efforts, rejecting the offer of help from Apex, were rather less likely to be reconvicted than those accepting Apex's services; the latter group were generally less likely to get jobs on release from prison (Soothill 1974: 153). This suggests that it is employment that counts rather than the services of the scheme. An MSC-sponsored *Action Research Programme for Disadvantaged People* (MSC 1976) in the mid-1970s consisted of six pilot schemes for different disadvantaged groups. One was a workshop for ex-offenders which was studied by the South Yorkshire Probation

Service's Research Unit. Little evidence was found of any effect on criminality and a high level of reconviction was expected.

Such results are the more surprising because of the existence of a strong and well-documented association between unemployment and recidivism. The opening chapter of this book considered the possible link between unemployment and crime. One aspect of such a relationship is the probability that those who have already offended are more likely to offend again if unemployed. Whereas the research on some aspects of the unemployment-crime relationship is ambivalent and even contradictory, when it comes to recidivism and unemployment the findings are more consistent. In one study after another it has been shown that probationers, ex-prisoners, and others are significantly more likely to re-offend at some later date if they are unemployed (Evans 1968; Davies 1969; Martin and Webster 1971; McLintock 1976; Home Office 1978; Softley 1978; Phillpotts and Lancucki 1979; Gormally *et al.* 1981; Farrington and Morris 1983; Harraway *et al.* 1985). This is true even when one takes into consideration the possibility that those who are most likely to be reconvicted are also those who are least likely to get jobs (Evans 1968; Gormally *et al.* 1981). Of course unemployment is not the only consideration. Studies of factors related to recidivism have found that, although unemployment is one of them, there are others, such as family and peer group influences, even more strongly associated (Buikhuisen and Hoekstra 1974; Phillpotts and Lancucki 1979; Farrington and Morris 1983). And, of course, reconviction is not an infallible measure of re-offending. Even so, in the uncertain world of crime and criminology an association between unemployment and recidivism seems to be one of the stronger contenders for certainty.

If unemployment is related to recidivism, then why is it that employment schemes have not been able to demonstrate a reduction in reconviction? The logic looks simple enough: if offenders are more likely to re-offend if they remain unemployed, then employment schemes should reduce re-offending. Such an assumption has probably been implicit, if not explicit, in most of the schemes that have been established. Extrapolating from this, it is also likely that a similar logic has been applied with regard to unemployment and crime in general, with the result that employment programmes have been seen as part of a response to the crime problem. This was true of the early United States programmes. However, the case is unproven. There are a number of possibilities.

The first point to make, however, is that employment schemes for offenders are not alone in being unable to show that they reduce offending. The 1970s were a time of disillusionment generally for those involved in working with, or 'treating', offenders. Several studies, notably those of Martinson (1974) in the United States and Brody (1976) in this country, were taken to indicate that 'nothing works'. Regardless of whether the form of intervention studied was particular sentences, custodial regimes, social programmes, or more clinical measures, a lack of consistent treatment effects was reported. This may be little comfort for the champions of employment schemes. But they might point out, with some justification, that the conclusion is also grossly oversimplified. Not only were there some significant exceptions to the statement that 'nothing works', but the person most responsible for giving rise to the sweeping generalization later revised some of his conclusions (Martinson 1979). Others have also sought to revise the 'nothing works' doctrine (Thornton 1987) and, as Walker points out, 'an equally justifiable inference from the evidence would have been that "nearly everything works" – but to more or less the same extent' (Walker 1987: 82). As far as employment schemes are concerned, rigorous studies of whether or not they reduce offending are pitifully few. The ones referred to earlier are now dated and are confined to special projects rather than the more general MSC schemes. It could therefore be argued that the conditions for determining whether employment schemes reduce crime have yet to be satisfied, and that until they are it is too early to reach any conclusions.

There are several possible explanations why studies have so far not found a reduction in reconvictions, and might fail to do so in future. One is that employment and training schemes are simply not the same as 'proper jobs' and therefore should not count as employment. This is an explanation consistent with the finding that recidivism is lower amongst those in full employment than amongst other offenders. In that case, studies of employment schemes need to distinguish between those who go on from the schemes to get jobs and those who do not before analysing follow-up reconviction rates. Such a study would, of course, need to take account of the fact that those who get jobs might be in some way different from those who do not. They may, for example, start off with more advantages, such as a better education, or have spent less time in prison, or have stayed on the scheme longer. It may also be that the overall level of unemployment is more important as a factor in offending than what is done about particular individuals.

Another possible explanation for finding no effect may be that re-offending has nothing to do with unemployment *per se* and everything to do with the lack of income that is associated with it; that the relationship is really between poverty and crime and being unemployed is associated with poverty. If this is the case then it is easy to see why, amongst those known to be predisposed to offending, employment schemes are not the answer, since they usually involve low levels of remuneration. This is a line of thinking that has been picked up by certain sections of the media who have suggested that YTS trainees, for example, commit offences as a result of the low level of the training allowance (*News on Sunday* 3 May 1987: 30). It finds some support from one of the few studies of work, crime, and income that has reported positive results. The Transitional Aid Research Project (TARP) in the USA was a large-scale experiment which set out to see if recidivism amongst a group of former prisoners could be reduced by offering them financial aid for up to six months after their release. The experimental group were compared with a control group on a number of factors, including the length of time they were employed after release. After a one-year follow-up, 'The assumption that modest levels of financial help would ease the transition from prison life to civilian life was partially supported' (Rossi, Berk, and Lenihan 1980: xix).

Ex-prisoners who received financial aid under TARP had lower re-arrest rates than their counterparts who did not receive benefits and worked comparable periods of time. Those receiving financial aid were also able to obtain better-paying jobs than the controls. However, ex-prisoners receiving benefits took longer to find jobs than those who did not receive benefits. Thus, those receiving payments generally worked less during the post-release year (Rossi *et al.* 1980). It should be noted that the system of benefits for the unemployed and for ex-prisoners is different in the USA to the UK. None the less, the TARP experiment was guided by the notion that poverty leads to property crime, and therefore invites consideration of causal mechanisms. If participation in employment schemes does not reduce reconviction but money does, then this suggests that there is more to reducing offending than simply making work for idle hands.

Employment schemes may also fail to influence offending because they are essentially short-term in nature; even so, many of those who start on them drop out before they complete the full period. It may not be reasonable to expect that attending a scheme for a few months can have more than a marginal impact on the background and experiences of a lifetime that have led a person to become an offender in the first place. For some of the greatly disadvantaged young people who are found in penal establishments (see, for example, Thornton, Curran, Grayson, and Holloway 1984: Ch. 2) participation in a well-run project may be one of the few positive experiences of their lives and may, along with other factors such as simply growing older, help to sow the seeds of a new way of life. But employment schemes alone or, indeed, any other kind of scheme, may not be capable of reversing the conditions that give rise to offending. If, as suggested at the end of Chapter 1, crime is a product of a range of factors in combination, with lack of employment being only one factor, then it may be that reducing crime also depends on achieving the right combination of conditions; addressing one problem alone will not provide the answer. A much broader attack on the conditions that give rise to crime may be necessary.

Similar considerations apply to that other criterion of success for employment schemes: getting a job. As noted earlier, the Apex Trust's project achieved little in this respect. Marris and Rein, in their study of employment projects established in the USA in the 1960s, in part as a response to delinquency amongst the young, concluded that employment schemes were powerless to achieve very much if the social and economic conditions in which they operated were not conducive to their aims.

The picture that has emerged so far is a dismal one and leads to the inevitable question: if employment schemes for offenders neither reduce offending nor produce jobs, then what is the point in having them? There are several ways in which this can be answered. First, as pointed out earlier, it may be that the research to date does not enable one to conclude that employment schemes do not work. If, as Walker (1987) contends, one might as well conclude that, on the evidence available, they work to the same extent as anything else, then clearly much would be lost if there were no schemes (and more might be gained presumably by having more of them). But there are other reasons for having them which are not based on reconviction rates. In a civilized, caring society, it may be argued, simple humanitarian concerns demand that ex-prisoners and other offenders should be given every assistance to rejoin society and not just be left to the mercy of market forces. On these grounds offenders should at least have as much access as other members of the community to such provision as there is, and they may need it more than most. The low level of educational achievement of a high proportion of offenders means that if they are to compete in the job market on equal terms, then some positive efforts have to be made to offset their disadvantages. This was recognized by a former Home Secretary:

> Some may question whether it is right that extra and specialised assistance should be given to offenders seeking jobs. Some would argue that this gives them an unfair advantage over non-offenders. It would certainly be difficult to justify this being done. But this is not what is happening. We see the offender as in need of special help not to give him an unfair privileged position, but

simply to equalise his chances in the increasingly competitive job market. (Leon Brittan, speech to Apex Trust, 12 December 1980)

It might also be argued that part of the value of employment schemes for offenders lies in their community-based nature. This is beneficial in two ways. First, for participants at risk of receiving a custodial sentence, schemes may broaden the options before the courts and offer the prospect of a non-custodial sentence being accompanied by something more positive in the nature of work and training than is likely to be found in a penal establishment. Given the findings reported in the previous chapter this is an important consideration. Second, community-based employment schemes offer a chance for offenders to be brought into a working relationship with the community that is beneficial to both sides: the offender may do some useful work for the community and other people in the community gain an opportunity to see beyond the popular media stereotype of offenders. Finally, if, as argued earlier, the need is to address the wider social and economic conditions which give rise to crime, then employment and training schemes for all, including those who have been convicted for offences, are an indispensable part of such a strategy.

Towards evaluation

Employment and training schemes are likely to be around in one form or another for some time. They are also, whether intentionally or not, going to involve those who have been in trouble with the law, if for no other reason than that offending is a widespread activity in our society. By the age of 28 nearly a third of males have been found guilty of at least one criminal offence (Home Office 1985a). The question is not, therefore, whether there should be such schemes but rather what they should be trying to do, what form they should take and how they might be improved. Thus there is a need to re-assess expectations about what employment schemes involving offenders can achieve. They are unlikely to provide a complete solution to either crime or unemployment. But, in conjunction with other measures, they have a role to play in responding to both.

This, in turn, means re-assessing how such schemes should be evaluated. Evaluation can take different forms. The controlled experiment is the most satisfactory method where one is seeking to attribute a specified outcome to a particular cause. But it is not the only method of evaluation and, as much of the literature on evaluative research demonstrates, it is often neither feasible nor justified (see Marshall *et al.* 1978). Measures like the level of re-offending and the number of participants going on to full-time employment are important, but so are other considerations and criteria, such as what the individuals and the community get from such schemes. As earlier parts of this chapter have shown, programmes like YTS and CP are not principally intended as regimes for treating offenders; nor are they, of themselves, capable of creating jobs. The starting point for any evaluation, therefore, should be a well-documented analysis of what schemes are trying to do and how they are doing it, rather than to assume that such things are known. Evaluation may therefore be defined as the presentation of systematically acquired information within a coherent framework, which enables those with an interest in the object of study to form their own conclusions. The study described below is of this kind.

The evaluation of schemes run by NACRO

Between the beginning of 1984 and the end of 1986 the Leverhulme Trust funded NACRO's Research Unit to undertake a study of the organization's Youth Training and Community Programme schemes. This study, the Employment and Training Evaluation Project, reflected the organization's wish to ensure that the work of its schemes was recorded, so that lessons could be derived from them. The brief of the research team was first, to describe the schemes and their operation; second, to evaluate the benefits of the schemes for the participants and the community and, finally, to influence the development of future practice and policy towards provision for disadvantaged unemployed people.

The project was not in a position to study the Youth Training Scheme and the Community Programme in general, and the research was therefore designed as a case-study of the role of a non-statutory agency, NACRO, in delivering national employment and training programmes. It was intended to document part of an important development of recent years so that useful conclusions could be drawn.

The project consisted of three parts. The first involved studying the objectives of the schemes as seen by different parties involved in them, including the government, MSC, NACRO, and participants. The second part looked at what the schemes were actually doing. Finally, the study examined the extent to which the schemes could be said to be achieving their stated objectives. Several research methods were used. Recording systems were developed in conjunction with the NACRO Sections running the YTS and CP schemes. These produced statistical data covering the state of the schemes month by month (numbers of starters and leavers, occupancy levels, and the age, sex, and ethnic group of participants) and some more detailed information about all participants who had passed through the schemes. In addition to this statistical monitoring system a variety of documentary sources was studied, including White Papers and other documents published by the government, MSC papers and reports, and material produced by NACRO, both centrally and by the schemes. Interviews were carried out with NACRO staff at all levels of the organization, with the staff of other agencies (MSC, Probation and Social Services, and the Careers Service) and with participants. Finally, two national surveys of all the YTS and CP schemes run by NACRO were carried out in order to obtain information which could not be acquired by other means. The first survey enquired into the background of the scheme managers and their perceptions of their schemes' objectives. The second asked for information about certain aspects of the work of the schemes.

An important part of the project involved four local area studies. At the time NACRO ran some 150 individual schemes in all parts of the country, providing places for up to 20,000 people, and it would have been impossible to study every one in detail. Four geographical areas were therefore selected for special study. They were chosen, after profiles had been drawn up of areas where NACRO schemes operated, to reflect different geographical locations and differences in economic conditions. In each area there was at least one NACRO YTS and one NACRO CP scheme. Although there was no expectation that the schemes would be 'typical' or 'representative', it was felt that these local area studies would give the researchers an opportunity to examine the dynamics of scheme operation, to look at the local context in which schemes operated, and to obtain certain detailed information which was not possible on a larger scale. The methods of statistical and documentary analysis and interviews already mentioned were applied in the local area studies and thus it was possible to establish how the local area schemes compared with the rest of the NACRO YTS and CP provision. In addition there was the opportunity for observation work and for following up participants after they left schemes. The four areas are referred to by initials which indicate their general location and are briefly described in Table 4.2.

Before looking, in the next chapter, at the YTS and CP schemes themselves it is necessary to describe the development of NACRO's employment and training services for offenders.

NACRO and its employment and training schemes

The National Association for the Care and Resettlement of

Table 4.2 A brief description of the four local areas studied

Area NE – a town in the North-East of England known for its heavy engineering and manufacturing industries. These industries had declined in recent years, and as a result unemployment had risen by two and a half times since 1979. The percentage of unemployed in mid-1984 stood at 17.8 per cent, well above the national average at that time of 12.6 per cent. Young people had been particularly badly affected.

Area SL – an area in South London which spreads from the former industrial riverside and dockland in the north of the area to the residential suburbs of outer London in the south. The area is a mixture of inner city decline and surburban prosperity. Employment used to be concentrated in the riverside area, but had fallen away with the decline of manufacturing industries and dock-related activity. Unemployment for London generally in mid-1984 was 10.2 per cent.

Area SW – an area of South Wales where the main industries were coal and steel production. The decline in these industries had given rise to high unemployment. In mid-1984 unemployment in the area stood at 15.2 per cent. About a third of the population lived in the one large town in the area.

Area WM – part of the West Midlands conurbation. The main industries were steel and heavy and light engineering, with the emphasis on manufacturing components for the motor industry. However, all these had been in decline in recent years, resulting in a level of unemployment in mid-1984 of 16.7 per cent.

Offenders started in 1966, following the report of the Advisory Council on the Treatment of Offenders on the organization of after-care for released prisoners (Home Office 1963). Previously after-care had been done on a voluntary basis by the National Association of Discharged Prisoners Aid Societies, a federation of local benevolent societies which, among other things, ran hostels for homeless ex-prisoners. NACRO was conceived as a successor to NADPAS which would continue to speak on behalf of local voluntary effort at a national level. But it was given the additional brief of seeking to develop new initiatives in working with offenders and those who, by nature of their background and circumstances, might be at risk of offending. The original intention was that NACRO should pilot new initiatives in the expectation that, if successful, they would be developed on a more general basis. It was 1972 before NACRO established any projects of its own. The first was a housing venture for the single homeless based in Manchester (LANCE). Like many subsequent NACRO enterprises this was not exclusively for the use of convicted offenders, for several reasons. It reflected NACRO's brief to cater also for those 'at risk' of offending, and it recognized the fact that being a known offender was often a matter of circumstance and whether or not one had been caught. Moreover, 'labelling theory' (the idea that labelling people as delinquent confirms them in this identity) was in vogue at the time and it was felt that to restrict projects to offenders only would perpetuate people's perception of themselves as criminals.

More projects followed quickly. There were more housing projects, education projects, a project for juvenile offenders and some work schemes, all within two or three years. The 1970s and 1980s saw a considerable development of NACRO's work, not only in running projects but in the development of provision in the community generally and in its information and policy work. At the same time the structure of NACRO changed from a regional one to a more centralized one with Sections, under a Section Head, responsible for particular areas of work. The increasing scale of NACRO's employment and training provision, principally through MSC funding, has been an important feature of the growth of the whole organization. The first employment project, a workshop in Manchester, stemmed from the first housing project when it was recognized that in the resettlement of offenders, particularly those who had been in prison, having somewhere to live and having work went very much hand-in-hand, and it was often difficult to get the one without the other. The Onward Workshop, as it was called, was primarily concerned with encouraging those who, even during a period of relatively low unemployment, had been out of work for some time to 'regain the work habit' in a sheltered environment. This 'Phase I model' was followed a year or two later by a Phase II, now funded by the MSC rather than the Home Office, and placing more emphasis on normal modes of production, manufacturing and renovating furniture on a non-profit basis for DHSS clients. Two more Onward Workshops were developed, one in Liverpool and another in Newcastle-upon-Tyne.

As unemployment increased during the 1970s, and with it the programmes for the unemployed, so NACRO became more involved in sponsoring employment measures, running a small number of projects under the Job Creation Programme (JCP) and the Special Temporary Employment Programme (STEP). At the same time NACRO became increasingly concerned about the impact of unemployment on communities, in addition to the resettlement of the individual offenders in those communities. In a response to the MSC's document, *New Special Programmes for the Unemployed: the Next Steps* NACRO stated that,

> Permanent employment opportunities need to be generated in the areas most blighted by urban decay and for the people most affected by structural unemployment ... which exists alongside the cyclical unemployment which the MSC's programme of temporary employment and training opportunities aims to alleviate. (NACRO 1977)

Even so the focus of the response was on people who were 'difficult to employ' and it was felt that the objective should be for participants in the programmes to be 'able to move on subsequently to permanent employment' (NACRO 1977: para. 2.4). The hope was also expressed that sponsors of the programmes would be able to 'test out a wide range of ideas and learn many lessons'.

A significant development occurred when JCP was replaced by the Youth Opportunities Programme. NACRO put forward proposals to set up an Employment Development Unit which would generate a small number of schemes, initially six, geared to the needs of young offenders. The *Application to the Area Board of the MSC* (NACRO 1978) indicated a number of objectives:

- To ensure that the programme was delivered to a difficult to reach group. (para. 1.3)
- To enable young people with adverse backgrounds to break out of a cycle of delinquency and involvement with institutions. (para. 1.2)
- To divert young offenders from custody or facilitate their early discharge. (para. 3.4)
- To assist the trainee in finding a full time job. (para. 3.8)

It was also stated that, 'Training and further education will play a prominent part in the overall scheme' (para. 3.9).

A slightly later document, *An Employment Project for Young People at Risk* (NACRO 1979: para. 1), commented that it was 'clear that many (YOP) sponsors find it difficult to cope with the demands made by youngsters at the harder end of the delinquent spectrum'. The proposal was concerned 'not only to open up opportunities but to ensure that these are acceptable in quality and style to the youngsters concerned' (para. 5).

Thus the 1970s saw a shift from the development of schemes whose principal focus was rehabilitating ex-prisoners and other serious offenders, towards an increase in provision which also reached a wider range of unemployed people. But there was a desire to gear schemes to the needs of individuals and to provide opportunities for them to move on to permanent employment. The Employment Development Unit subsequently became the Section of NACRO that ran NACRO's YOP and, later, YTS schemes. Meanwhile the Onward Workshops were becoming incorporated within another Section that first ran the Community Enterprise Programme and then the Community Programme.

NACRO'S objectives

The objectives of the programmes as a whole were set at a national level by the government and the MSC, as described earlier. However, there is considerable scope for interpretation at each stage of their translation into operational reality. Official definitions of aims are often no more than broad statements of intent, leaving room for much detail to be filled out by those with management responsibility at central and local levels. Both YTS and CP have been delivered throughout the country through a chain of management. As one evaluation of an experimental regime for young offenders has put it: 'The conversion of policy into reality, therefore involves a chain of command in which the policy intentions may be variously interpreted at each stage' (Thornton *et al.* 1984: para. 3.3).

Government-sponsored employment schemes were delivered, in fact, through more than one chain of command. First, there was the MSC which had both central and local bureaucracies. Then there was the range of agencies – private employers, local authorities and non-statutory bodies – who actually ran most of the schemes. NACRO was one of these, with its own particular interests and reasons for running the schemes. In addition to NACRO's aims, as interpreted and operationalized by its central management, local staff had to take account of local circumstances and conditions.

In general NACRO's primary objective was to secure the delivery of provision and resources to people who were disadvantaged in terms of competing in the labour market: to ensure that those who most needed employment and training did not miss out on what was available. The concern was that without special provision by an agency like NACRO, offenders and other disadvantaged groups would find it hard to secure places on YTS and CP schemes and would get left even further behind in the competition for training and work. The belief that offenders were disadvantaged in gaining access to jobs and, indeed, to many employment schemes run by other agencies, was supported by a survey of YTS providers which found that: 'A number of schemes did not accept young people facing particular problems or disadvantages. Schemes responsible for one fifth of Mode A trainees did not accept either those with learning difficulties or ex-offenders' (Department of Employment 1985: 309).

Closely associated with this primary objective was a second one: that of trying to ensure that the schemes were equipped to meet the needs of such a disadvantaged group without becoming labelled as inferior to other YTS and CP schemes. This meant maintaining a good quality of provision, giving participants a positive experience, and ensuring that the schemes were accepted by the local community in which they operated. It also meant offering more support and guidance to individual participants than was likely to be found on many other schemes. Although it was not a stated objective of the programmes nationally, the NACRO schemes placed some emphasis on their potential for furthering participants' personal and social development by offering courses in basic skills, and a high level of staff support and counselling. Whilst formal training was accorded a high priority in YTS and, as far as possible, in the Community Programme, the emphasis was on the acquisition of broadly based, rather than job-specific, skills. As it was put by a clothing manufacturer with whom NACRO sought to place participants: 'You get them into good work habits; we'll teach them how to sew pockets on.'

NACRO attached an increasingly high priority to the pursuit of equality of opportunity in its work. This was both an aim in its own right and was in accordance with the first objective, since black people, as well as offenders, are liable to experience higher than average levels of unemployment and are particularly likely to be affected when unemployment rises (Showler and Sinfield 1981: 10; Hawkins 1984: 61, 66).

Obtaining full time employment was seen as the most positive outcome for participants and schemes did aim to equip them to compete for jobs. However, it was also recognized that because of the employment situation, together with participants' lack of previous qualifications and other disadvantages, including a history of offending, a substantial proportion would find it hard to obtain jobs when they left. The schemes therefore sought to develop participants' options in various directions, including further education and training, and by trying to prepare them to survive without a job. With regard to offenders, schemes were noticeably cautious, recognizing that the role they could play in reducing further offending was a limited one. The goal is probably best characterized as one of containment in the community, and this had two facets. First, it was hoped that, by offering offenders the opportunity of constructive activity, the schemes might increase the chances of an offender remaining in the community rather than going into custody. Second, the hope was that, by occupying a person's time in a meaningful way, one might increase the chances of young people in particular reaching a period in their lives when they were less likely to commit offences, and achieving this with the minimum of damage to themselves and others. There were considerable variations in the way that these objectives were perceived. Schemes in areas which had been particularly badly hit by unemployment were likely to be much less optimistic about participants getting jobs when they left than those in less affected areas. Generally speaking NACRO staff were more cautious about the likelihood of participants staying out of trouble and getting jobs than were the participants themselves.

Two points are worth noting about the objectives of the NACRO schemes. First, they were as much concerned with the way the schemes were run as with any long-term outcomes. Second, they were expressed in terms of the needs of individual participants, in contrast to the way the objectives of the government and MSC were expressed, which tended to focus more on the needs of industry, commerce, and the economy. This is not to say that there was necessarily a direct conflict between the objectives of NACRO and those of the MSC, but there was definitely a difference in emphasis. In addition to meeting the criteria set down by the government and the MSC, NACRO sought to add its own dimension. In operational terms NACRO's schemes were always expected to respond to the demands of central government policy and to avoid pursuing more specialized objectives at the expense of national requirements. Although individual schemes in theory had to serve two masters (NACRO and the MSC), it was understood throughout that, once due allowance had been made for lobbying and for negotiation over differences, the MSC was the final arbiter of scheme implementation and programme delivery. Nevertheless a certain tension was inevitable between the broadly-based remit of the programmes and the special concerns of an agency devoted to pursuing the interests of a particular group. This is unlikely to have been an experience peculiar to NACRO. Wherever there are large scale programmes there will be concern from various quarters to ensure that certain interests are not neglected. It is therefore important that such programmes are designed to take account of the wide range of needs they are likely to encounter. It is also important that adequate consultation takes place with all who have a legitimate interest in representing different sections of the population, not only when programmes are conceived, but when they are modified subsequently. NACRO's concerns regarding employment and training were set out in its response to the *New Training Initiative* (MSC 1981a and b). Replying to the MSC's consultative document, NACRO stated,

We have three major concerns:
(i)   NACRO is concerned about the prevention of crime and the creation of a social climate which discourages the growth of crime and anti-social behaviour.
(ii) NACRO has always worked with disadvantaged people who have a range of special difficulties – and we would wish to ensure that any new arrangements took these special difficulties into account.

(iii) As a non-statutory organisation which has accumulated considerable experience in working across and bringing together the statutory and non-statutory sectors we are anxious that any new organisational arrangements should preserve the flexibility of the current MSC Special Programmes. (NACRO 1981b)

The response went on to emphasize that training must be related to future employment or disillusion and alienation would result, that special provision was needed for those with special needs and that the needs of the disadvantaged should be met in all parts of the initiative. NACRO subsequently sought to pursue these general concerns in the more specific contexts of the Youth Training Scheme and the Community Programme.

Chapter five

The schemes in operation

NACRO's Youth Training Schemes

Development

NACRO's youth training provision had started with the Youth Opportunities Programme schemes set up by its Employment Development Unit from 1978 onwards. With the advent of the New Training Initiative and YTS, NACRO set out the role it hoped to play in the Initiative. This was to be based on its experience during YOP:

> When we began in 1978 to develop YOP for offenders our rationale was simple. We were aiming to prepare disadvantaged young people from the criminal justice system for jobs in the normal economy. In our first year of operation over half the trainees who left our schemes did so to take up full time jobs. Since then the employment prospects for 16–21 year olds have worsened considerably and the predictions for the near future make our original simple aim untenable. One vital lesson to be learned is that we must establish an honest partnership with the young people who come to our projects and must be realistic about their future employment prospects. (NACRO 1981c: 8)

NACRO's proposal to run a network of YTS schemes identified three specific objectives:

> First, to provide a training programme which will enable trainees to compete for such jobs as are available in the normal economy and to compete confidently with some hopes of success. Further, to enable trainees to take advantage of training or education opportunities which are available in the general provision.
>
> Second, to provide a training programme of intrinsic interest and relevance to the lives of trainees and which deals with matters relating to their lives now and in the immediate future.

Third, to provide within the training programme opportunities to take, in collaboration with the appropriate agencies, whatever steps are possible to resettle the trainees in the community and to help them lead their own lives free from conflict with the law. (NACRO 1981c: 16)

A significant development for NACRO was the issuing by the Youth Training Board in 1983 of a paper, *Equal Opportunities in YTS for Young Ex-Offenders* (MSC 1983c). This stated that YTS,

could be a valuable factor in helping in the resettlement of young offenders and ... should result in a measure of achievement which would do much to increase confidence and lift young offenders out of the rut of failure and disillusionment ... (but) only if special help is given in meeting the needs of this group of young people. (MSC 1983c: para. 4)

The paper concludes, however, with the statement that, 'the Youth Training Scheme is not a re-settlement programme for young ex-offenders' (para. 8).

The following year, 1984, saw cuts being made in the number of Mode B places under YTS and NACRO responded to this by arguing the need to ensure continued access to the scheme for young offenders. Its submission to the House of Commons Employment Committee (NACRO 1984: para. 3) restated NACRO's concerns:

The reasons for NACRO becoming involved in YOP in 1978 stand today. First it was felt that disruptive and disadvantaged young people from borstal, detention centre or local authority care would have difficulty finding places on most YOP schemes and would need special help which NACRO could give. Secondly, schemes set up in run-down and crime-ridden neighbourhoods would provide for young people from such areas an alternative to vandalism and petty crime.

In April 1985 the government announced that YTS was to become a two-year programme, leading to a recognized qualification. As part of the discussion that preceded this announcement NACRO produced a paper, *Learning the Job* (NACRO 1983d), which reflected the organization's continuing concern with what the schemes should be about. This stated that the future development of NACRO schemes should focus, as far as possible, on providing:

Experience and training relevant to the stated needs of our young people in terms of them entering the world of work ... (because) both YOP and YTS have been and now are about providing work related training rather than treatment for delinquency or resettlement. (NACRO 1983d: para. 2.3)

The paper continues,

There has been considerable debate within our staff groups as to whether we are in the training business or ... the resettlement business. We have tried to resolve this creative conflict by asserting we are in both businesses as caring trainers. It is our job to ensure young people can come on to a NACRO YTS and get a chance to participate in an exciting programme which they would not get if we did not offer it. (NACRO 1983d: para. 2.5)

The document reflects a belief that not only should the organization deliver the schemes to those who might not otherwise have such opportunities, but it also has to add something more which is relevant to the particular needs of the young people it deals with:

But we have consistently insisted that we aspire to provide Youth Training as set out by the MSC. To this we add the NACRO element which is simply to provide each and every trainee with a high level of personal support according to the wants and needs, perceived and expressed by the trainees, as far as we can. (NACRO 1983d: para. 2.4)

Thus NACRO's response to that part of the New Training Initiative relating to the training of young people reflected its concern to ensure access to training by the most needy, a desire to provide training relevant to their needs and aspirations and, it may be noted, a gradual lowering of expectations over the years that training would necessarily lead to jobs.

The documents that have been cited do not necessarily reflect the complete NACRO perspective, however, since scheme staff and participants had their own views. Scheme managers saw the main aim as helping participants to get a job, but they also had other concerns. Foremost amongst these were the provision of education opportunities, helping participants to become more independent and helping them acquire basic life and social skills. Less prominent were their concerns to provide job-related training and to help trainees to stay out of trouble with the law whilst on the scheme. Within the schemes, other staff tended to stress the importance of their relationship with trainees:

They've [trainees] been in an institution; they've been in care. Some of them have had to do community service or youth custody ... They don't have to be here ... I think it's really important, their relationship with their peers and the staff – that they're individuals and they're treated with respect. (a Scheme Supervisor)

The evolving nature of government-funded employment and training for young people has already been outlined. The rapid changes to the programmes had important implications for the administration of the schemes, the constraints within which they had to operate, and their ability to meet the needs of certain groups of young people. The most significant change in programme arrangements since 1983 included:

- completing the adjustment from YOP to YTS, including a shift down the age range towards 16 year olds;
- coping with restrictions on the number of places available under Mode B of YTS to enable a greater emphasis on employer-based schemes in Mode A provision;
- preparing for the tighter framework of YTS2, including occupancy-related funding and competence-based training assessment.

These changes created a stressful environment at scheme level and added to the problems of promoting the personal and social development of a difficult group of trainees. It is widely believed that young people with difficult and disturbed backgrounds need the chance to acquire more enduring values and models of behaviour in a stable environment if they are to achieve a socially acceptable transition from childhood to mature adulthood. Although changes in the programme may have been justified, the uncertainty and stress resulting from the manner of their introduction worked against providing such conditions and, hence, against the interests of the trainees.

The number of NACRO YTS schemes increased from the six first set up by the Employment Development Unit in 1978-9 until, in the financial year 1983-4, there were 33 NACRO YTS schemes with 2,059 approved places, 1,551 of them filled, an occupancy rate of 78 per cent. The total cost of the schemes was £4.6m and the cost per place that year, £4,513. This compared with a cost per place for Mode B1 schemes in general of £3,600. By 1985-6 the total cost was £6.8m for 44 schemes with 2,120 approved places, 1,578 of them filled, an occupancy rate of 79 per cent. The unit cost, per filled place had fallen to £4,040, which compared with £4,500 per filled place for Mode B1 nationally. These are not the true costs of the schemes, since trainees would have been in receipt of benefit had they not been on a scheme. When the estimated costs of benefit are allowed for, the true additional cost to the Exchequer for the NACRO schemes was £3,140 per filled place in 1985-6.

Recruitment to the schemes

Recruitment to YTS was through the Careers Service. However, many referrals to NACRO schemes came about initially as a result of some other form of contact. In particular, since NACRO aimed to cater for offenders, it was keen to encourage probation officers, working both inside and outside prison, and social workers working with juveniles at risk, to arrange through the Careers Service for their clients to be placed on a NACRO scheme. There were in fact three main 'gateways' to the NACRO YTS schemes: first, referrals from the Careers Service itself; second, referrals originating with the Probation or Social Services; and third, contacts originating with young people themselves, as a result of hearing about NACRO schemes through friends or relatives or through independent contact with the staff. These last were collectively termed self-referrals.

Referrals originating with Probation and Social Services staff declined consistently over a period of years. In particular the proportion of Probation Service referrals fell from around 33 per cent during YOP in 1982-3 to 14 per cent in 1985-6. In part this reflected the shift to a younger age group with the change from YOP

Figure 5.1 NACRO YTS recruitment, 1983-6

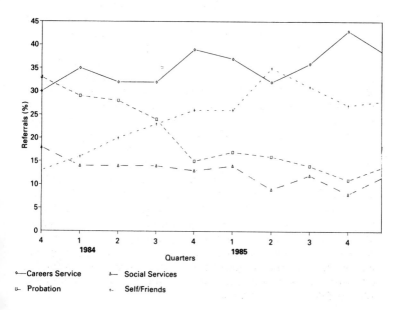

to YTS, with more 16 year olds coming on schemes, and Probation Services tended to have less contact with juveniles. There was some compensating increase in recruitment through Social Services Department social workers. But even so there was a continuing decline in both Probation and Social Service referrals once the transition from YOP to YTS was completed, falling from 43 per cent of all referrals in the first quarter of 1984 to 26 per cent in the same quarter of 1986 (see Figure 5.1).

Meanwhile, recruitment resulting from direct personal contacts with young people increased from 16 per cent to 28 per cent of all trainees over the same period, having peaked at 35 per cent during 1985. For most of this time the proportion of referrals initiated by the Careers Service remained more or less stable at around 35 per cent. But during the early months of the two-year YTS framework this also was proportionately greater, rising to 49 per cent, while the figure for referrals by Probation and Social Services staff had sunk to 15 per cent.

The significant thing about the decline in the proportion of social work referrals is that NACRO schemes looked to this source, and the Probation Service in particular, as the main means of recruiting offenders. It was not surprising, therefore, to find that a shift away from this source of recruitment was accompanied by a reduction in the proportion of young offenders joining the schemes. This declined from around 70 per cent in 1983–4, when YTS succeeded YOP, to just under 60 per cent in the later part of 1985. In particular it was reduced during the early months of the new two-year YTS framework, which came into effect during the closing stages of the study, in 1986. During the first three months of the new framework, fewer than half of all the trainees recruited (48 per cent) were known to have been convicted of an offence in court prior to joining a NACRO scheme. To some extent the proportion of convicted offenders has been affected by the growing use of cautioning for young people. But even when this is taken into account, the figures for mid-1987 showed that only just over half (54 per cent) of the NACRO trainees on two-year YTS had been convicted and/or cautioned.

During the period the schemes were being studied, on average approximately two-thirds (63 per cent) of all NACRO trainees were white males aged 16 or 17 who had left school during the preceding year with no recognized qualifications and little, if any, previous work experience. The proportion of young females was small (14 per cent), but this reflected the limited numbers of females amongst those dealt with by the criminal justice system. The proportion of young black trainees (16 per cent) was approximately three times the proportion of black trainees found on YTS as a whole. Many of the young people had experienced a disrupted family background and almost half of all the trainees (46 per cent) were subject to the care or supervision of statutory welfare agencies when they joined. In many cases, their previous record of education and training had been erratic. Seventy per cent had no qualifications when they joined, compared to 21 per cent on YTS nationally (Table 5.1).

Whilst this shows that NACRO YTS schemes were indeed catering for disadvantaged young people, these averages conceal some important variations. The change in the proportion of young offenders on the schemes was paralleled by other shifts in the characteristics of participants. At the same time that the proportion of offenders on the schemes was declining, so was the proportion with no qualifications. An earlier study of NACRO's schemes (Crow and Richardson

Table 5.1   Characteristics of YTS trainees: comparative analysis, 1985–6 (%)

	NACRO[1] YTS	All[2] YTS
Sex		
Male	86	52
Female	14	48
Ethnic group		
White – European	83	96
Black – Afro-Caribbean	12	2
– Asian	2	1
Other/No information	3	1
Educational qualifications		
None	70	21
CSE/Other qualification	15	31
'O' Level or above	3	48
No information/Results awaited	12	–
Residential care		
Experience of Community Home/Fostered	24	–
Previous convictions		
No convictions	38	–
Convicted, no custodial sentence	40	–
Convicted, at least 1 custodial sentence	19	–
No information	4	–

Notes: 1. Analysis of NACRO YTS based on 2,686 trainees who left schemes between May 1985 and March 1986.
2. Analysis of all YTS schemes drawn from results of MSC's follow-up survey of trainees who left schemes between April and September 1985 (MSC 1986).
(– = Information not available).

1985: Appendix I) reported just over 80 per cent of trainees with no qualifications; by 1985–86 the proportion was nearer to 70 per cent. Changes in the characteristics of the trainees recruited cannot be automatically linked with changes in the means of recruitment, however. Much depended on how the various gateways functioned in different parts of the country. The extent of the variations is indicated in the regional analysis set out in Table 5.2.

Many NACRO schemes in the North of England and South Wales consistently had a higher than average proportion of socially and educationally disadvantaged young offenders amongst their trainees. In some locations, such as Area SW where the scheme was studied in detail, this was achieved by sustaining a high proportion of referrals of known offenders from Probation and Social Services staff. But in most northern areas, such as Area NE, it was achieved with a recruitment process which centred on referrals initiated via the Careers Service. Schemes in the South of England, on the other hand, and to some extent those in the Midlands also, were less likely to attract a majority of young offenders within their trainee groups. In many instances, such as Area WM, this was the result of a recruit-ment process which relied substantially on direct personal contact with young people. But in other locations, including Area SL, it happened where recruitment depended as much on referrals initiated by Careers Services staff as it did in northern areas.

The manner in which various gateways functioned was reflected in the views expressed by trainees about how and why they had joined NACRO schemes. In the two local area study schemes which had recruited a higher than average proportion of young offenders, at least one-third of the trainees concerned had further court appear-ances pending when they joined. In personal interviews, they cited preparation for these and the advice of Probation and Social Services staff as a major factor in their decision to join:

> My Probation Officer said I should go on the scheme. I had another court case coming up and I had a better chance of getting a lighter sentence if I came up here.

> I had to go to court so I had to get a job ... my Probation Officer suggested I should get on the NACRO scheme ... it was the quickest one to get on.

Other young offenders said that they already knew some of the young people working on the schemes and this contact with 'their own kind' made them feel comfortable about joining. In the two schemes recruiting proportionately fewer trainees with previous convictions, the incidence of outstanding court appearances was lower: less than one-fifth. Trainees on these schemes more often said

Table 5.2 Referral and recruitment sources of NACRO YTS trainees: analysis by region and previous offending record, 1985–6 (%)

Referral/recruitment	All Trainees	North		Midlands		South		London		S. Wales	
		Non-offenders	Offenders	Non-offenders	Offenders	Non-offenders	Offenders	Non-offenders	Offenders	Non-offenders	Offenders
Careers Service	37	45	45	38	34	42	30	43	17	22	13
Probation Service	14	4	17	1	19	2	27	1	15	19	58
Social Services	11	4	12	4	12	5	14	6	19	15	24
Self/friends/relatives	31	44	19	53	29	42	25	37	24	37	4
Other sources	8	4	6	5	6	9	4	13	24	7	1
Per cent of non-offenders/offenders in each region		(30)	(68)	(46)	(52)	(41)	(56)	(48)	(51)	(18)	(79)
(Base nos)	(2,565)	(297)	(686)	(360)	(401)	(102)	(139)	(204)	(219)	(27)	(122)

Note: Analysis based on 2,687 trainees who left NACRO YTS schemes between May 1985 and March 1986. 122 records were excluded because of missing information.

they joined because they were attracted by the kind of activities offered, or because they had friends who had joined and said the schemes were worthwhile.

In this context it seems reasonable to suggest that the reduction in the predominance of known offenders amongst NACRO's trainees was the result of something more complex than a simple shift from one recruitment gateway to another. The most likely explanation is the changing nature of YTS itself; in particular the advent of YTS 2. This saw schemes move away from a position where they could concentrate on recruiting a carefully defined client group, with support from other agencies, towards one where they had to provide an approved training programme which could be open to a wider range of young people. Its effects appear to have been most visible in the South of England. It would be wrong to exaggerate the extent of the changes; it remained the case that throughout the first half of the 1980s, the NACRO Youth Training Schemes catered for a high proportion of people who, by any criteria, would have had difficulty competing in the labour market. None the less, what occurred during that period was a move from the very open and flexible structure of YOP, which tolerated creative innovation, to a YTS which became increasingly structured and demanding. It seems that, however desirable such a shift may have been in itself, the NACRO experience indicates the dangers attendant upon such changes in policy and the need to ensure that broadly based programmes do not neglect certain groups.

The work of the schemes

Nation-wide statistics and more detailed local observations showed that the schemes provided trainees with a mixture of activities in workshops, specific work projects, and placements with individual employers, all of which focused on job-related skills, as required by the design of the programme. The schemes supported these with a range of opportunities for young people to develop their personal competence in matters such as literacy, numeracy, and inter-personal communications. The statistics also showed that there were no significant differences in the type of activities undertaken by male and female trainees or by black and white trainees, but male trainees and white trainees were more likely to have had some experience of all three types of training. A summary of the extent of the activities undertaken is set out in Table 5.3.

Most of the skill-related training centred on traditional manual craft trades. Where trainees took part in workshops, most were geared to the building, painting, and decorating trades. Mechanical

Table 5.3 Training activities undertaken by NACRO YTS trainees:
analysis by sex and ethnicity, 1985–6 (%)

	All trainees	Males	Females	White	Black
Main training programme					
Workshop (s) only	36	37	36	36	41
Workshop (s) + project (s)	11	11	10	12	7
Workshop (s) + placement (s)	22	22	29	22	25
All three	16	18	8	18	12
Other combinations/ missing information	15	12	17	12	15
Supplementary activities					
Personal effectiveness/ development	55	54	60	54	61
Day-release course	13	13	16	14	8
Literacy + numeracy tuition	32	33	26	30	43
Computer literacy	50	51	44	51	47
Residential training package	24	24	19	25	19

Note: Analysis based on 2,687 trainees who left NACRO YTS schemes between May 1985 and March 1986.

engineering, catering, and office skills were the other most common occupations covered. Placements also focused on building, decorating, and motor vehicle work, although overall they provided work in a wider range of occupations than did workshops. In four out of every five cases (79 per cent) placements were with small firms which employed no more than ten people. Trainees who took part in schemes in the North of England were significantly less likely to move from workshops into placements than those on schemes elsewhere, even though there was no significant difference in the length of time they stayed on a scheme.

Shifts in the training took place over time. For example, the use of groups as a means of external training, following on from internal workshop-based activities, was reduced to a point where it was no longer available for most trainees. The growth of workshops was itself a major shift from the focus on on-site work experience, which predominated in pre-YTS times. Some element of computer literacy rapidly became a feature of the training which was taken up by a majority of those recruited, whilst basic literacy and numeracy tuition remained a component for about one-third of all trainees throughout the study period. The procedures used for assessing the

Table 5.4   Length of stay and activities undertaken by NACRO YTS trainees: analysis by region and previous offending record, 1985–6 (%)

	All Trainees	North		Midlands		South		London		S. Wales	
		Non-offenders	Offenders	Non-offenders	Offenders	Non-offenders	Offenders	Non-offenders	Offenders	Non-offenders	Offenders
Length of stay (in weeks)											
1–4	10	7	13	7	9	6	9	9	10	11	12
5–13	23	22	22	17	29	20	27	30	29	14	15
14–26	22	18	24	20	21	27	23	21	29	25	21
27–39	13	14	13	13	14	13	15	10	12	18	15
40 or more	31	38	29	42	26	34	25	30	21	32	37
(Average stay in weeks)	(27)	(30)	(26)	(32)	(25)	(29)	(25)	(26)	(23)	(29)	(30)
Training activities											
Workshop(s) only	36	44	50	21	33	10	21	35	51	25	25
Workshop(s) + project(s)	11	14	12	13	13	14	19	1	2	11	13
Workshop(s) + placement(s)	22	21	17	27	16	28	14	41	34	39	25
All three	16	17	14	21	21	24	27	9	5	–	18
Other combination/missing information	15	5	8	19	17	26	19	15	8	25	20

Supplementary activities											
1. Personal effect-iveness	55	66	66	40	26	71	74	63	66	73	64
2. Day-release course	13	2	3	27	28	18	12	12	5	43	24
3. Literacy + numeracy tuition	32	31	22	32	26	44	45	43	54	54	36
4. Computer literacy	50	56	51	49	55	74	59	40	38	39	48
5. Residential	24	25	29	20	23	17	27	22	17	23	28
(Base nos)	(2,565)	(297)	(691)	(365)	(406)	(102)	(139)	(203)	(219)	(28)	(122)

progress and competence of trainees underwent a parallel process of change to accommodate the programme's demands for more formal testing.

Differences also emerged when the activities of NACRO's schemes in various parts of the country were compared with one another, as set out in Table 5.4. These findings for the year 1985–6 demonstrate that, once the offending background of the young people recruited was allowed for, there were no significant differences between the four largest regional groups in terms of the trainees' length of stay with NACRO. There were, however, substantial differences in the patterns of their training. In particular, the proportion of trainees taking part in northern schemes who trained solely in scheme-based workshops was roughly double that found in most other regions. Elsewhere the schemes relied to a greater extent on various combinations of external training which involved projects and, more often, individual placements with employers. The only exceptions to this were schemes in London, which focused more directly on the provision of workshops followed by placements. A similar picture emerged during a survey undertaken in mid-1986. At that time schemes in the North of England and South Wales had only 28 per cent of their trainees on average placed with employers, whereas in the Midlands and the South the proportions were 43 per cent and 60 per cent respectively.

In all four of the schemes from different regions which were studied in detail, the staff made efforts to establish a form of personal contact with their trainees which went beyond the formal terms of their commitment to provide training and work experience with YTS. This was expressed in their concern to create sympathetic day-to-day supervisory relationships and working conditions; their consistent provision for reviewing personal progress or problems in an informal manner; and their flexible use of disciplinary procedures. Measured by the responses of young people themselves, it seems that these efforts were usually successful and won respect from most of the trainees concerned. A majority of those who commented in personal interviews or postal questionnaires said that they had found taking part in the scheme helpful and that they had found working relationships to be fair and satisfactory. The difficulties which were mentioned most often by trainees and staff centred on two problems: first, lack of interest and consequent absenteeism amongst a minority of trainees who in effect 'contracted out' of their schemes efforts and disrupted the general atmosphere; and, second, disappointment and frustration amongst some trainees whose expectations about placements were not fulfilled, as in the case of one trainee who expressed it thus: 'I want to go on a placement, but so far I've been let down two or three times. They say they'll work something out but then they can't do it.'

During 1984–6 substantial numbers of NACRO's trainees took part in activities which were intended to promote their personal and social development in addition to the main elements of job-related training. Fifty-four per cent were given specific help in improving the effectiveness of their personal and social skills and, if the responses of trainees are anything to go by, with some success:

> I seem more grown up now I've been here. I used to do stupid things; I don't now. If I'd been sitting here a year ago, I'd have been nervous about this sort of thing [the interview], but I'm not now.

> When I first came on the scheme I started acting like a big kid. I didn't know the people ... but you get new mates and I've grown up more ... You still mess about but I feel I've become more mature.

A range of other informal sessions or more structured courses were also taken up. Basic literacy and numeracy, computer literacy, short residential packages and day-release arrangements were each undertaken by up to one-third of all trainees. These figures remained more or less constant throughout the study period, except for a rapid rise in the proportion of trainees participating in computer literacy work, to more than half by 1986.

Assessing trainees

The assessment of individual trainees' progress gained increasing importance over the years. Under YOP, the emphasis had been on trainee-centred reviews, using methods like log-books maintained by young people themselves. As YTS established itself, and particularly in anticipation of the shift to YTS 2, more formal procedures and universal standards became the norm. The NACRO schemes followed this trend, using a variety of ways of assessing the progress and competence of trainees. Procedures centred on a more or less common core of arrangements throughout the country, but each scheme had its own local framework and variations. The methods consisted primarily of induction tests, weekly assessment reports by workshop or placement supervisors, quarterly reviews by senior Training Organisers, and oral reports on trainee groups to staff meetings, often supplemented by log-books kept by trainees. In 1986, with the need for more formal testing emerging in the two-year programme, two-thirds of NACRO's schemes reported making regular use of specific task-related tests with their trainees. Greater standardization of these procedures evolved during the ensuing months in order to satisfy the MSC's demands for more effective measurement and certification of YTS trainees' achievements.

Assessment procedures used in the four schemes studied in detail illustrated the differences between individual schemes. All four made use of weekly supervisors' reports and trainees' log-books as some part of their procedures. Three of the schemes had instituted quarterly reviews by Training Organisers and some form of induction assessment or task-related tests during training. But other procedures, such as written reports from supervisors on trainee groups and case-conferences on selected (usually difficult) trainees were used in only two schemes. The staff of the schemes shared a general view that the formal role of assessment procedures as measures of progress was secondary to their usefulness as a means of promoting helpful supervisory relationships with trainees. In their evaluations of progress, therefore, they focused as much on the trainees' acquisition of basic work routines, such as time-keeping, self-discipline, and team work, as on their learning of more specific skills. This was epitomized by a staff member from the scheme in area SW who said, 'You don't rush them. You let them take their time so they know what they're doing and you try to get success as a team because that stops them getting at you or at each other.'

The trainees' own assessments of their experiences and progress were generally positive. Their comments showed that most found their schemes to have been a helpful way of learning more about practical skills, such as painting and carpentry. This was often the sort of thing they had expected to get from participation in the schemes when they joined, and in this respect their expectations were largely fulfilled:

> The painting's been most useful. I enjoy it. When I first came here I thought it was rubbish, but after a few weeks I started to enjoy it.

> I've learned a lot because I didn't get much out of school. But here you learn about painting and decorating and things like that, all what's needed and how to do it ... I learned more here than on [a previous YTS scheme], I've had a lot more experience here.

The only reservations which trainees commonly expressed concerned the limited possibilities for being able to put their skills to the test in placements within real working environments (which applied particularly in Areas NE and SW), and the fact that what they had learned did not take them far enough to receive recognition for having a full trade skill. They shared this latter concern with many of their supervisors.

An important factor in assessing what trainees got out of being on the schemes is the length of time they were actually there. Between 1984 and 1986 just under half of the trainees (45 per cent) stayed with their schemes more than six months, the average length of stay in 1985–6 being 27 weeks. This figure, which was much the same in different parts of the country, was somewhat lower than the average length of stay in YTS as a whole (36 weeks). The faster turnover of NACRO's trainees exerted some constraints on the effective planning and delivering of training, but was only a more acute form of a problem experienced by YTS schemes in general.

Within this context, records for 1984–6 indicate the emergence of a settled pattern of participation in training activities by the young people joining NACRO's schemes. Nearly all trainees (85 per cent) initially spent time in workshops on the schemes' own premises. For one in every three trainees (35 per cent) this was the only setting they experienced before leaving, where they stayed for an average of 14 weeks. But approximately half of all trainees (49 per cent) were able to supplement this with experience of external placements or (less often) projects, so that on average they spent 16 weeks within the scheme and 20 weeks in training and work experience activities else-where. As one might expect, the longer trainees stayed the greater the chance that they experienced a range of different training activities and settings. Fourteen weeks seemed to be a crucial turning point: trainees who stayed longer than this were likely to have a much better chance of taking part in a wider range of activities. Some changes in this pattern emerged with the transition to a two-year programme during 1986, with an increase in the use of individual placements.

Young offenders

Reference has already been made to variations in the proportion of offenders taking part in the NACRO Youth Training Schemes. Overall, however, NACRO's schemes worked with substantial numbers of young people who had been in trouble with the law and included amongst these was a significant minority of persistent and serious offenders. During the study period, on average three-fifths (61 per cent) of the trainees passing through NACRO YTS schemes were young people who had court convictions before they joined. Of these young offenders, just over a quarter (27 per cent) had four or more convictions and one-third had served some form of custodial sentence, usually in a detention centre.

The statistics also show, as illustrated in Table 5.5, that trainees

Table 5.5 Length of stay and activities undertaken by NACRO YTS
trainees: analysis by previous offending record, 1985–6 (%)

	All trainees	No convictions	Convicted, no custodial sentence	Convicted + custodial sentence
Length of stay (in weeks)				
1–4	10	7	10	14
5–13	23	21	22	30
14–26	22	21	24	24
27–39	13	13	13	14
40 or more	31	38	31	19
(Average stay in weeks)	(27)	(30)	(27)	(21)
Training activities				
Workshop(s) only	36	30	39	47
Workshop(s) + project(s)	11	11	12	10
Workshop(s) + place-ment(s)	22	29	21	16
All three	16	17	18	13
Other combinations/ missing information	15	13	10	13
Supplementary activities				
Personal effectiveness	55	55	56	53
Day-release course	13	15	12	9
Literacy + numeracy tuition	32	34	32	25
Computer literacy	50	50	52	44
Residential training package	24	21	26	22

Note: Analysis based on 2,687 trainees who left NACRO YTS schemes between 1985 and March 1986.

who had a limited record of offending before they joined stayed as long as other young people who had no record of convictions. Consequently, they received a similarly varied training programme, subject to local circumstances. The same cannot be said, however, with regard to those with a record of more persistent or serious offences. Trainees who had already served custodial sentences for previous convictions and who had further court appearances outstanding were most likely to have left their schemes early, without moving through the different training activities available. Most of them undertook training in scheme-based workshops, supplemented by personal effectiveness sessions. But the proportions moving on to placements or undertaking other activities such as day-release courses and literacy and numeracy tuition were low by comparison with other trainees.

Only part of the difference in training experienced can be explained by reconvictions resulting in further custodial sentences. Only 20 per cent of those with previous custodial experience left as a result of being taken into custody again during their stay. The largest number of these young people decided to stop attending of their own accord, without any known alternative employment or training to go to. This was true of almost one-third of those with previous custodial experience (31 per cent) compared with less than a quarter (24 per cent) of the others with a record of convictions.

More than one-fifth (22 per cent) of all NACRO's trainees had a court appearance pending when they started, with most of those concerned having previously been convicted of other offences. More than 40 per cent of these cases were known to have resulted in a non-custodial sentence, with a further 40 per cent still waiting to be determined when the trainees left their schemes. However, because neither details of the offences nor other reliable data for comparisons were available, it is difficult on this information alone to offer any assessment of the extent to which having attained a place on a NACRO scheme had any direct influence on the outcomes of outstanding court proceedings. But in a survey of schemes undertaken in mid-1986, staff reported that assisting trainees appearing in court was a significant, though not large, part of their work. Approximately one in seven of all trainees made a court appearance during the three month period examined in the survey. Scheme staff submitted or contributed to over 200 court reports associated with these hearings, and in over 50 cases attended in person to support the trainee. The staff further reported that, in more than one-fifth of the cases heard, attendance at a NACRO scheme was referred to by the courts as an acknowledged factor in determining a non-custodial sentence. To the extent that this was an accurate assessment, it offers some evidence that the schemes had played a part in keeping young offenders in the community.

Between 1984 and 1986, 20 per cent of all NACRO's trainees were charged with or convicted of offences alleged to have occurred while they were taking part in the scheme. Such charges or convictions were most common amongst those young people who had four or more previous convictions (34 per cent reconvicted in 1985–6) and amongst those who had already received a custodial sentence before joining NACRO (36 per cent reconvicted in 1985–6). Since these trainees were unlikely to have stayed with NACRO for more than six months, and many left much earlier, the schemes had only limited opportunity to make much impact on more than a small number of persistent offenders. A third of all such cases known to have been dealt with resulted in custodial disposals, with more than half of those previously sentenced to custody (51 per cent) receiving a further term. A more positive picture was presented by those trainees who previously had only a limited record of convictions and avoided any further charges during a prolonged stay of six months or more in YTS. During the study period, they constituted almost one in eight (12 per cent in 1985–6) of all NACRO's trainees and one-third (32 per cent) of those who joined with a conviction but no previous record of custody.

The staff of the four schemes studied in detail made it clear that they did not have high expectations of the impact which their work might have on the behaviour of their trainees. In particular, there was common agreement that during their stay much depended on how trainees used their leisure time and that any influence was likely to be limited once trainees had left NACRO. The trainees themselves were usually more optimistic. Approximately two-thirds of those interviewed in the four schemes felt that working with NACRO reduced the chances that they would get into trouble with the law, largely because they had more money as a result. But those who thought they were unlikely to find further employment and pay after leaving were less hopeful. The results of surveys which followed up trainees from the four local area studies during the year after they had left tended to confirm the reservations expressed by the staff rather than the optimism of the young people. In three of the surveys, more than half of those trainees who had been convicted of offences before joining NACRO were known to have been reconvicted within a year of leaving (56 per cent, 60 per cent, and 50 per cent). In one instance, Area SL, the incidence of reconviction was lower, at 30 per cent. Seven per cent of trainees without a record of convictions when they joined NACRO were convicted subsequently.

It is difficult to infer cause and effect in such matters, but it seems that the impact of the schemes was most visible in the extent to which they were able to deliver training and work experience to young people with a limited record of court convictions. Those young people whose criminal record had been sufficiently serious or persistent for them to have received a custodial sentence before coming on YTS had greater difficulty in attaining the same level of achievement.

Employment and training after YTS

During the period of the study approximately one-quarter (24 per cent) of the trainees on average were known to have moved directly on to a job or to further education and training (excluding other YTS schemes) when they left. This was substantially less than the 59 per cent for YTS nationally reported by the MSC in its follow-up survey of all YTS leavers for a comparable period (MSC 1986). Given the backgrounds of the young people concerned, this is not surprising. It is, perhaps, more surprising that the proportion remained more or less constant throughout the period, when recorded unemployment rates showed deteriorating labour market conditions in most parts of the country. As it was, almost half the trainees leaving NACRO's schemes during this time (46 per cent) were known to have become unemployed. Black trainees were less likely to move on to a job or further training (20 per cent) than white trainees (25 per cent).

Further analysis of 1985–86 leavers' destinations in relation to the length of time they spent with NACRO shows that (with cases involving missing information discounted) moving on to a job or further training was almost as common amongst those trainees who left before their allotted time (27 per cent) as it was amongst those who completed a full period of training (32 per cent). This experience appears to be a common one in YTS as a whole and was apparent throughout NACRO's schemes in different parts of the country. Most of the minority who found employment at the end of a full period of training (20 per cent) moved into jobs with employers who had provided placements as part of the NACRO programme. But those who found employment at a point earlier in their training were more likely to move into jobs unconnected with their schemes.

Once again there are differences between schemes in different regions. Taking the information available in 1985–6, the proportion of trainees moving into jobs or further training in the North of England (18 per cent) was half that recorded in London (36 per cent) and in the South outside London (34 per cent). Comparable figures for trainees in the Midlands and South Wales lay in between (20 per cent and 27 per cent respectively). These differences were not accounted for by variations in trainees' personal characteristics (other than offending record) or in the lengths of time which trainees spent with schemes in the regions concerned, although more trainees in London tended to leave early than elsewhere. The differences were, however, associated with variations in local market conditions, as indicated by employment rates for the travel-to-work areas in which the schemes were located.

In all regions, the proportion of trainees with court convictions before joining NACRO who went on to jobs or further training when they left was markedly less than the corresponding proportion of trainees who had no previous convictions. The figures were especially low amongst those trainees who had served custodial sentences prior to joining, as shown in Table 5.6. Because of the regional variations

Table 5.6   Proportion of NACRO YTS trainees[1] moving on to further
employment and training[2]: analysis by previous offending
record and region, 1985–6 (%)

	All trainees	*No convictions*	*Convicted no custodial sentence*	*Convicted + custodial sentence*
Region				
North	18	24	17	14
Midlands	21	26	19	13
South	34	43	27	25
London	36	44	31	23
South Wales	27	50	24	16
All regions	24	32	21	16

Notes: 1. Analysis based on 2687 trainees who left NACRO YTS schemes between May 1985
and March 1986.
2. The proportion of trainees recorded as moving on to 'further employment and training'
does not include those moving to other YTS schemes. During the period in question,
these amounted to only 4% of all trainees and to less than 5% of trainees in each
region. It should be noted, however, that the proportion moving to other YTS schemes
was generally greater amongst trainees with no convictions (6%) than amongst those
with convictions, whether they had received only non-custodial sentences (4%) or had
experience of custody (2%).

which existed, however, the proportion of young offenders with prior
experiences of custody who left schemes in the South to move to jobs
or further training (25 per cent) was almost double that in the North
(14 per cent). It was also higher than the proportion of northern
trainees with no convictions who moved to jobs (24 per cent).

NACRO's schemes made a variety of arrangements to help
trainees search out new opportunities after they had left. In the 1986
survey referred to earlier, almost all schemes reported that they gave
trainees personal assistance in completing job applications, time off
to visit the Careers Service, Job Centres and other employment
agencies, and training in job-search and interview techniques. More
than half the schemes also said they arranged for advice on benefit
entitlements and personal welfare matters (such as family disputes,
contraception, or drug abuse) to be available to trainees preparing to
leave.

Measured by the extent to which some ex-trainees were able to
find and sustain employment after leaving NACRO's schemes, it
seems that the efforts made by the scheme staff met with a degree of
success. But often this only meant obtaining temporary jobs or places
with other MSC-supported employment and training programmes.
This was demonstrated in the follow-up surveys of young people who
had left schemes in the four areas selected for detailed study. Within

roughly one year of leaving about half of these ex-trainees had taken up some form of employment and this was more or less consistent throughout the four areas. In none of the four, however, were more than one-third still in employment at the time of the follow-up survey itself and many of the jobs had been held for only short periods of time. Moreover, amongst trainees from the North and South Wales, virtually all of the employment recorded consisted of places on MSC-supported programmes such as CP or Community Industry. Only amongst those ex-trainees in the South and the Midlands (Areas SL and WM) were significant numbers in jobs at the time of the surveys (20 per cent and 29 per cent respectively).

The perceptions of this situation by NACRO's staff and by trainees were realistic and well-informed. They accepted that the chances of employment for young people after leaving were probably no better than even. Staff were concerned about trainees who left early without any positive options to pursue, and considerable effort was devoted to finding local placements so that at least some young people might find these an effective stepping stone into work. But staff felt that there were limits to their capacity to do more than make training available as a means of keeping their young workers in touch with the demands of the labour market. Most of the trainees interviewed were undeterred either from declaring that they would aim to find some form of work, or from attaching some value to the activities they took part in during their time on the schemes. Many saw their training as providing experience and as being helpful in enabling them to undertake work for themselves or for other people on a casual basis, such as painting their houses or repairing motor bikes and cars.

Summary

NACRO's Youth Training Schemes succeeded in recruiting a high proportion of socially disadvantaged young people, many of them with a record of offending, and many of these quite persistent young offenders. However, as the schemes became more structured in their training there was a relative decline in the proportion of more difficult and disadvantaged entrants. The schemes provided a variety of job-related training opportunities in workshop settings and individual placements with employers. A range of supplementary activities directed mainly towards personal development, literacy, and numeracy was also available and was taken up by substantial numbers of young people. Scheme staff sought to establish a more personal contract with their trainees than that formally required by the training programme and to include within it flexible assessment procedures and supportive supervisory relationships. This situation was appreciated by most of the trainees who joined, including many who had been convicted of offences. There were two main points of concern, however. First, up to one-third of the trainees left within three months, thereby reducing the effectiveness of any benefits that might accrue from the training and support. Second, the availability of placements was greater in the South of the country than in the North.

The main consequence of training on NACRO's schemes was to help trainees establish some contact with employment or further training. But the extent to which this happened varied with local labour market conditions and with the trainees' offending backgrounds. Much of their subsequent employment was of a temporary or casual nature, and in many northern areas it depended almost entirely on other MSC-supported programmes. And in all parts of the country, young offenders who left the schemes faced a substantially greater prospect of prolonged unemployment than those who left with no record of convictions. A survey by the Department of Applied Economics at Cambridge University found that, where a job exists, those who have been on a YTS scheme are more likely to get it. It may, therefore, be argued that by delivering YTS to a group of disadvantaged young people, the NACRO schemes are at least enabling them to participate in the effective re-distribution of jobs to ex-YTS trainees (Deakin and Pratten 1987).

NACRO's Community Programme Schemes

Development

Some form of provision by NACRO for unemployed adults started with the Onward Workshops referred to earlier. It was with the advent of the Community Enterprise Programme in the late 1970s that the provision changed from small, one-off projects to a more broadly-based programme involving a network of schemes offering 2,000 places. The controversy surrounding the replacement of CEP by the Community Programme prompted NACRO to consider any involvement in CP carefully and to issue a *Statement of Policy on CP* (NACRO 1982) and a background paper for its staff explaining NACRO's position. Both documents said that, whilst NACRO regretted the replacement of CEP by CP, it was important to ensure the continuation of such provision as was available for those who would otherwise have few options. At the same time, it was necessary to sustain a commitment to certain conditions. These included attempting to ensure that as many of the places as possible went to offenders (especially those coming out of prison) and those at risk of offending, improving the quality of life in needy areas, and the delivery of good quality training to participants. When the MSC produced its consultative document, *Towards an Adult Training Strategy* (MSC 1983a), NACRO responded with a policy document, *Unemployment, Training and Resettling Ex-Offenders* (NACRO 1983c) which expressed the view that the Adult Training Strategy 'must be geared to meet the needs of the unemployed as well as the employed' and must serve the interests of individuals as well as those of the economy. It stated, 'The objectives of our Community Programme Schemes are to provide opportunities for long term unemployed people, many of whom have an offending background, and other people from disadvantaged areas to work in schemes of community benefit' (NACRO 1983c: para. 6).

The document also urged that there should be a training component in CP to enable the long-term unemployed to participate fully, and that such a programme needed to be part of a comprehensive adult education strategy. There was also concern about the disruption and discontinuity that programmes had suffered in the past and it was argued that to be effective CP needed continuity and stability. A moratorium on the development of places, which was imposed on the Programme in the first year of its operation, was not helpful in this regard.

Subsequently, the main developments in that part of CP run by NACRO, as for CP in general, were concerned with its expansion. NACRO's initial involvement was at the level that it had previously been under CEP, 2,000 places. By mid-1984 NACRO was managing 7,083 places on 80 schemes throughout England and Wales, and by June 1986 the number of filled places had increased to 17,408 on 120 schemes and NACRO had become the largest single managing agent for CP, providing 7 per cent of the national total of places and 15 per cent of places available in the voluntary sector. The majority of schemes (60 per cent) were in the Midlands and North of England, with just over a quarter (27 per cent) in the South, including London, and 13 per cent in Wales (Table 5.7). The budget needed to run the schemes also increased substantially each year, from an expenditure of £15.3m in 1983–4 to £43.1m in 1985–6. The cost of a NACRO CP place was around £4,400, similar to that for other CP schemes. As with YTS the real cost, taking account of benefits payable, was less and was estimated at an average of £3,000 a year.

Not surprisingly the development of such a large-scale operation had a considerable effect on what had, barely a decade before, been a small voluntary organization employing fewer than a hundred people. The Community Programme Section became by far the

117

Table 5.7 Unemployment and the distribution of CP places, England & Wales (Oct/Nov 1986) (%)

| Region | U/E Rate | Propn. of U/E out of work > 1 year | Distribution of CP places: | |
			National	NACRO[1]
South East	8	37	7	7
London	9	40	8	7
South West	10	34	8	13
E Midlands & E Anglia	9	39	9	8
W Midlands	13	47	13	19
Yorks & Humberside	13	42	13	17
North West	15	45	18	8
Wales	15	42	10	13

Source: Cols 1 and 2, Department of Employment (1987); col. 3, from MSC data; col. 4, from NACRO data.
Note: 1. 'Best fit' comparison with MSC data.

biggest part of the organization, and management structures and administrative systems had to be substantially altered to cope with the fact that NACRO had now become a large employer. Although sheer scale was an important feature of NACRO's development of CP, the organization's Director was concerned to remind those involved that size was not everything:

> It is not enough to have lots of schemes with lots of places and these places filled. What we need to be able to say is that on every scheme, each person is getting an opportunity to do something worthwhile, and an opportunity to learn something, to be trained to develop themselves if that is what they want. (*NACRO Staff Bulletin* no. 18 Dec. 1986)

Among scheme managers, staff and participants the schemes were seen as an opportunity for constructive activity and work experience as an alternative to the dole. The main concern was getting back into full-time employment and schemes were viewed as something that could enhance participants' employability, although it was recognized that the external job market severely restricted what was likely to be available. Two of the local areas studied (NE and SW), where the proportion of offenders on the schemes was high, focused on seeking to ensure that offenders had access to any employment opportunities available. The scheme managers regarded their task as, 'ensuring that we deliver the opportunities and the resources we've got in terms of jobs and money to the right clients, i.e. offenders' (a Scheme Manager). The two areas where the offender ratio was not so high (WM and SE) focused on providing occupational and employment skills training to people who were generally socially disadvantaged, of whom some were offenders. The emphasis of these schemes was on:

> enabling as many long term unemployed as possible to be fitted into a twelve month scheme with a prospect of getting them trained into the work effort ... and giving them a better chance at the end of twelve months of getting a job. (Scheme Manager)

Other scheme staff saw their objectives in terms of getting people back into the 'work habit' and providing a year's employment.

Most of the participants interviewed regarded the schemes as simply being a year's work. Those who were promoted to full-time status or to charge-hands hoped their extra responsibilities would enhance their chances of employment after CP. Participants, whether offenders or not, said their main reasons for joining were 'to end the boredom of unemployment' and 'to earn a regular wage'. Those who joined in areas where unemployment was particularly high often added that there was no other work available to them. They regarded their participation as work for a year rather than as part of any long-term plan which might enable them to gain full-time permanent employment.

Recruitment to the schemes

There were several criteria for entry to the Community Programme. To be eligible for the programme a person had to be aged between 18 and retirement age and have been out of work, for twelve months if over 25 years old or six months if less than 25. CP schemes had to pay the local 'rate for the job' but, apart from the scheme managers and supervisors, the cost of wages (during 1985–6) should not exceed an average of £67 per person per week. Managing agents were required to offer to participants the same conditions of service and union agreements which operated within the agency itself. Furthermore the work done by schemes should not displace jobs or place at risk existing businesses and was to be of benefit to the community in which the scheme operated.

Compared with CP generally, those who came on the NACRO schemes were more likely to be male and under 25 years old. This probably reflects the emphasis on recruiting offenders, who are more likely to have these characteristics. The proportion of black people entering the NACRO schemes was also higher than on CP in general. NACRO participants were more than twice as likely as other CP participants to have no qualifications and a third had been unemployed for over two years. Just under 40 per cent had already

Table 5.8 Characteristics of NACRO CP participants and national CP participants (%)

	MSC Survey	NACRO 1985/86
Sex		
Male	77	84
Female	23	15
Age		
18 – 24 yrs	65	69
25 + yrs	35	30
Ethnic group		
White	93	88
Afro-Caribbean	7	10
Asian	–	1
Other	–	1
Length of time unemployed		
More than one year	57	62
Convictions		
None	–	48
At least one	–	47
Not known	–	5
Qualifications		
None (or not known)	25	59
CSE, 'O' level	37	24
'A' level or above	12	3
Other (incl. technical qualifications)	26	1
Vocational qualifications	24% of 'other'	
Previous experience of MSC programmes		
None	–	57
YOP/YTS	–	26
CEP/CP	–	9
More than one programme	–	1
Other	–	3
Not known	–	4

Notes: 1. Special Employment Measures Advisory Group data provided figures for 'sex-length of time unemployed'. The latter figures taken from the latest MSC survey of leavers November 1985.

2. The MSC included vocational qualifications with academic qualification (– = Information not available).

been on some kind of MSC programme, mainly YTS, but nearly one in ten had been on CP before. The distribution of places on the schemes between known offenders and non-offenders was nearly even, 47 per cent being known to have convictions, and the proportion remained at around this level throughout the period when the programme was expanding rapidly (Table 5.8). Almost a third (30 per cent) of the offenders were known to have been convicted of their last offence within the six months prior to joining.

As with YTS, recruitment was through different 'gateways'. Although official recruitment was through Job Centres, information was collected on how participants' first contact with the NACRO schemes came about. Job Centres themselves provided about half of all referrals (52 per cent) and approximately a quarter originated with the Probation Service. Almost a fifth of participants found out about the scheme from informal sources. Not all those with convictions were referred by the Probation Service: 52 per cent were referred by either Job Centres or came through informal contacts. Those referred by probation officers were more likely to be people who had been charged with or convicted of an offence a few months before joining CP. Offenders were significantly more likely to be recruited onto schemes in areas where unemployment was above the national average, especially Wales and the North of England. The local area studies illustrated the differences in recruitment. In Area NE one of the two CP schemes focused mainly on referrals from the local probation day-centre while the other, larger, scheme received probation clients from several area offices as well as referrals from other sources. Both schemes aimed specifically to provide places for offenders, and recruited above average numbers of people with convictions. In Area SW the scheme liaised with probation offices near to its project sites which were based in rural towns. As a result, both informal and local service links enabled it to recruit a large number of offenders onto those projects. By comparison the schemes in Areas SL and WM received referrals from both district Job Centres and probation offices. These schemes sought to cater for people who were socially disadvantaged in general (some of whom would have criminal convictions), rather than to focus on offenders in particular. This more diverse strategy resulted in proportionately fewer offenders being recruited.

The work of the schemes

The Community Programme focused on creating and supervising a range of work opportunities which provided benefit to the community as well as to long-term unemployed adults. Much of the

Table 5.9 Deployment of NACRO CP participants during 1985–6: offenders vs non-offenders by regions (%)

	REGIONS					
	North %		Midlands %		South %	
	Non Offender	Offender	Non Offender	Offender	Non Offender	Offender
Deployment						
Conservation/ reclamation	32	42	36	58	38	51
	38		46		43	
Community work incl Crime prevention and placements	14	9	11	3	17	5
	11		8		12	
Building/painting and decorating	20	26	23	24	21	36
	24		24		27	
Workshops	7	16	7	6	2	0
	12		6		1	
Administration	15	1	12	2	12	3
	6		7		8	
Other	12	5	12	6	9	4
	8		7		7	
Status						
Full-time	21	7	17	6	13	8
	13		12		11	
Part-time	65	84	61	75	75	79
	76		67		77	
Transferred, part to full-time	13	8	20	18	10	12
	10		19		11	
Other	0	1	2	1	1	1
	1		1		1	
Duration						
Average length of stay (weeks)	39	35	40	33	35	30
	36		37		33	

	London %			Wales %			All %	
	Non Offender	Offender		Non Offender	Offender		Non Offender	Offender
13	13	(13)	43	53	(49)	32	46	(39)
14	4	(10)	4	5	(4)	13	7	(9)
40	60	(49)	20	32	(27)	22	30	(26)
1	2	(1)	2	2	(2)	6	8	(7)
11	8	(9)	18	3	(10)	14	2	(9)
21	13	(17)	13	5	(8)	12	7	(10)
13	8	(11)	32	11	(20)	18	8	(13)
75	81	(79)	59	80	(71)	68	80	(74)
10	10	(9)	9	7	(8)	13	11	(12)
1	1	(2)	0	2	(1)	1	1	(1)
34	30	(32)	36	34	(35)	37	32	(34)

work was directed towards labour-intensive, manual tasks (such as environmental improvements and reclamation, building, painting, and decorating) and to providing services to 'vulnerable' groups in society such as the elderly, people with disabilities, and pre-school children. NACRO schemes incorporated a range of projects of which, in mid-1986, almost two-thirds were manual, labour-intensive (Table 5.9). Community benefit is difficult to define and almost impossible to assess and quantify without more precise definition: what constitutes the community and who in it benefits from what? The NACRO schemes did two types of work intended to benefit others: the provision of services and the production of commodities.

Services, often involving unskilled labour, were supplied to identifiable disadvantaged groups. This work included crime prevention projects, small-scale housing improvements on council estates, and laundry services for elderly people or people with disabilities. Such projects were sometimes constrained either by competing for work with other schemes, or by local politics. The production of commodities was usually managed along similar lines to a small manufacturing business, but without a profit motive. Examples included making or renovating furniture for DHSS claimants, converting halls into community centres, and converting ex-service buses into children's play buses. Such projects often required particular equipment or specific tools, but because they were not permitted to make a profit from the goods, resources for equipment were limited to funds that had been allocated to the scheme for this purpose.

Generally, projects involving the application of various trade skills were felt by scheme staff to be the most constructive in terms of providing benefits to both participants and recipients. The participants received a range of skill training and recipients received a tangible asset. By comparison, projects involving tasks like environmental clearance and reclamation work, or gardening, required fewer skills and were felt to be of more benefit to the recipient or to the local community than to the workers. A less tangible but not unimportant feature of the NACRO schemes was that they brought offenders into a positive relationship with the communities in which they worked. This was often commented on by the schemes and the staff of other agencies as being of benefit to both the offenders and the people they came in contact with, who were thus able to see offenders in a new and more favourable setting.

As a consequence of the wage constraints on CP managing agents described earlier, a lot of participants worked part time. It was sometimes possible, however, for a part-time worker to transfer to full time if someone who was doing full-time work left. Three-quarters of the participants on NACRO's schemes were employed part time. Opportunities to participate full time declined from 16 per cent of places in 1984-5 to 13 per cent by 1985-6, but in each year 12 per cent of participants transferred from part to full-time work. Because the rule meant that there was a relatively low limit to what any individual could earn on CP, the programme was generally less attractive to those with family commitments than to single people. This explains why a high proportion of those on CP generally tended to be young people. Since NACRO, in addition, sought to direct its schemes towards offenders (who also tend to be young) this may explain why the average duration of stay on the NACRO schemes during 1985-6, at 8.5 months, was rather less than the national average of 9.9 months.

Participants' experiences of the programme differed, depending on their sex and race. Most women worked in administration or welfare projects (64 per cent), whereas most men were appointed to projects involving manual labour (74 per cent) on conservation, building, or painting and decorating sites. Overall there was little difference between men and women in whether they worked part or full time, although on average women stayed slightly longer (9.25 months compared to 8.5 months for men). There was also a contrast between the experiences of black and white workers. Over half (56 per cent) of black participants were recruited to environmental or construction sites compared to two-thirds (68 per cent) of white people. Conversely more black people, mainly Asian, were appointed to administration and projects involving work in the community compared to white employees (24 per cent compared to 17 per cent). Black employees were proportionately more likely to work part-time (79 per cent compared to 72 per cent of white employees). Nevertheless black people remained on the schemes for approximately the same duration as their white colleagues.

The experiences of participants with convictions also differed from that of non-offenders. Over three-quarters of the known offenders were allocated to manual tasks compared to just over half of the non-offenders (see Table 5.9) and they were less likely to be appointed to administration or community projects. In addition people with convictions more often worked part time and left earlier than those with no convictions. Those who had at least one custodial sentence stayed the shortest time with NACRO (7.25 months on average) whereas those with no convictions remained longest (9.25 months).

The emphasis on certain types of project work varied throughout the country. The Midlands, South of England outside London, and Wales were heavily involved in environmental improvement, whereas London focused on building, painting, and decorating projects.

Workshops were more likely to be found in the North, and community work (including crime prevention and work placements) was most prevalent in the North, South and London. Community projects and workshops in the North were more likely to recruit offenders than elsewhere and offenders were more likely to work on administration projects in London than in any other area.

The proportion of full to part-time working also varied across the country, and may well reflect differing levels of economic activity. The average weekly wage on CP of £67 per week (at the time) would also be likely to affect the relative attractiveness of a job in different parts of the country. Wales had the highest proportion of full-time workers; the South of England and London had only half as many (Table 5.9). London had the highest proportion of part-time workers and the Midlands the lowest, although twice as many people working part time were given the opportunity of transferring to full-time work in the Midlands as anywhere else. There were also regional differences in the length of time people spent on CP schemes. Participants remained longest on schemes in the Midlands and North and the least time on schemes in the South and London.

Formal training on CP (as opposed to whatever knowledge participants acquired whilst on the job) could be financed in three ways. First, it could be funded by agreement with local MSC offices. Second, training could be funded from underspending from schemes' wages budgets. Third, it could be financed from operating costs allowances. During 1985–6 almost half (49 per cent) of the participants on the NACRO schemes received some formal training. Training arrangements varied considerably from scheme to scheme as well as from one part of the country to another. A survey carried out in mid-1986 showed that during the month of June schemes in the Midlands provided twice as much training as those in either the South or North. Most of the training was funded either from operating costs or from underspending from wages allocation. At the time of the survey London schemes were the highest spenders, with expenditure of £47 per session. Generally the South, outside London, spent half as much as London at £24 per head, other areas spending between £11 and £13 per head.

Participants' responses to training were mixed. A common view amongst participants at the time that they were on the schemes was that the value of training courses was limited because of the lack of opportunity, in many cases, to put new skills into practice. But in follow-up surveys ex-participants reported that they had found the training to be useful in building their confidence, developing their skills and widening their job prospects. For many participants, however, the main source of the learning whilst on CP came from being told how to do particular types of work by a project leader or supervisor. The quality of this direct, on-the-job instruction inevitably depended on the aptitude of the project leader or supervisor and it may be that more emphasis should be given to strengthening this kind of instruction. A third of schemes reported that they made skill- or task-related appraisals of their employees, most of the reports being completed by either personnel or training staff. Two of the five schemes in the local areas studied required supervisors to provide regular assessments of their employees. These assessments were regarded as being of value if or when a reference was required on the participant's standard of work.

Counselling or welfare advice was not formally part of the Community Programme. Nevertheless during 1985–6 three-quarters of the schemes supplied advice to their workers and almost a quarter (24 per cent) of participants received help with welfare problems. Participants commented on the benefits of being in work, such as being financially more secure and sharing problems and experiences with work colleagues. Some non-offenders believed that, by working alongside people with convictions, they dispelled many prejudices against offenders.

Adult offenders

Of the 47 per cent offenders taking part in the NACRO schemes, half had received at least one custodial sentence prior to joining CP. In 1985–6 15 per cent of the previously convicted offenders who joined had a court case pending when they started. Those who had received a custodial sentence in the past were more likely to be in this group (19 per cent) than those who had previously had only non-custodial sentences (11 per cent). Where the outcome of the court hearing was known (in 55 per cent of the cases) just over a third (34 per cent) received a custodial sentence, over half (56 per cent) were given a non-custodial sentence and a tenth of the cases were dismissed. Forty per cent of offenders (51 per cent of those with custodial experience and 29 per cent of the others) were being supervised by either the Probation or Social Services when they started work on CP.

The indications were that NACRO CP was being used by participants and the statutory services more as a post-sentence provision than as a means of minimizing custodial sentences. However, where schemes did seek to offer themselves as part of a non-custodial option, they appear to have had some success in influencing sentencing. The survey of schemes carried out in mid-1986 found that in one month (June) 161 participants were known to have made a court appearance. The schemes prepared reports for the

127

courts for half of these cases, and in 26 a member of staff appeared in court to speak on behalf of an employee. The schemes reported that in 35 cases working for NACRO was referred to by the court as an acknowledged factor in deciding on a non-custodial sentence for a CP worker. This represents 22 per cent of cases appearing before the courts that month.

Studies in the selected local areas served to reinforce the impression that statutory services were using NACRO CP as a post-sentence provision. People who were referred to schemes by their probation officers often sought either to earn money to pay off

Figure 5.2 NACRO CP trends, workers' destination, 1984–6

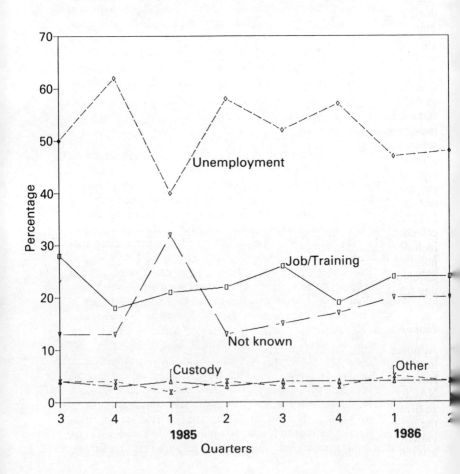

outstanding fines, or to obtain some constructive occupation which might reduce their chances of re-offending and breaching their supervision order. Offenders who were interviewed reported that participation on NACRO schemes gave them financial and personal stability as well as a regular day-time occupation. This was regarded as an attractive alternative to either 'doing nothing' or being tempted to return to crimes like theft or burglary. A few mentioned that work on CP helped them because they were paid weekly. Fortnightly unemployment benefit payments often meant that they regularly got into debt. Thus, a weekly wage enabled these workers to budget more effectively and to be able to pay outstanding fines more easily.

Overall, one in eight offenders (12 per cent) were reconvicted or reappeared in court on charges for offences alleged to have occurred during the time they were working on one of the schemes. This was more likely to occur for offenders who had previously served custodial sentences (15 per cent) than for those who had not (8 per cent). Further conviction or charge while an offender was taking part in a scheme varied considerably. For example, for the ordinary CP scheme in Area NE the incidence of reconviction was 24 per cent and in Area SW it was 19 per cent. However, in the workshop scheme in Area NE, which had almost 100 per cent offender participation, the incidence of charge or conviction known to occur whilst on the scheme was only 11 per cent. When followed up after leaving the schemes, 42 per cent of the workshop participants in Area NE reported having re-offended within six months to a year after leaving the scheme, compared to 29 per cent of those who had been on the ordinary CP scheme. In Area SW the self-reported re-offending rate 6–12 months after leaving was again 19 per cent. (Self-reported offending is not comparable to re-conviction since it is liable to include offences for which the person has not been charged.) It is not possible to easily explain these variations, which could be due to differences in the people going to the different schemes as much as to any feature of the schemes themeselves.

Employment and training after CP

Almost a quarter of all leavers (22 per cent in 1984–5 and 25 per cent in 1985–6) were *known* to go directly into a job or further training on leaving a NACRO CP scheme. Approximately half of those leaving NACRO schemes became unemployed and 4 per cent were known to go directly into custody. An important additional figure, however, is the proportion leaving where their 'destination' was unknown. This varied inversely with the proportion becoming unemployed on leaving (see Figure 5.2), suggesting that where the destination was unknown, it was likely that the people concerned had become unemployed. The MSC national figures for the destination of leavers from CP invariably omitted this important category. This artificially boosts the other percentages, including the one quoted most often by the government and MSC: the proportion going into jobs, which thus appeared to be higher than it actually was with the 'not knowns' included. If the 'not knowns' are omitted from the NACRO figures, then the proportion of participants going to jobs or further training on leaving increases from around a quarter to the same level (28–30 per cent) as for CP generally. Allowing for the fact that the NACRO participants were more disadvantaged in terms of competing in the labour market, this might be regarded as something of an achievement for those concerned.

There were variations in outcomes depending on how long participants had remained on CP, where they lived, and whether or not they had been convicted before joining. Participants were more likely to go into employment if they left early than if they remained for the full duration of a scheme, suggesting that those who stayed to the end of their allotted period tended to do so because they could not get anything else. Not surprisingly, people who left schemes in areas where unemployment was below average were more likely than others to find employment. Schemes in the North had the lowest percentage of people going directly into jobs on leaving (20 per cent) whereas the schemes in the South recorded the highest percentage (31 per cent). Similar variations occurred in CP generally (see Table 5.10). Those who worked in administration or community based projects had the best chances of moving into employment or further education and those in workshops had the least chance (Table 5.11). This may, of course, be a reflection of factors other than the type of work done. The people who found it most difficult to obtain employment were those who already had convictions (especially a

Table 5.10 Proportion of NACRO CP workers moving on to employment and training by region and previous offending record (%)

	Not convicted	Convicted	All NACRO	MSC (1985 Survey)
Region				
North	25	16	20	22
Midlands	40	33	23	28
South	35	30	31	35
London	34	30	21	38
Wales	36	34	28	25
All	37	32	24	25

Table 5.11   Destination on leaving CP by deployment whilst on scheme and time on scheme

	Destination				
	% Unemployment	% Education/ Job	% Other* (inc. custody)	% NK	% Total nos
Deployment:					
Project Type					
Conservation/energy	49	22	8	21	2,180
Building, painting and decorating	43	25	8	24	1,472
Community work, crime prevention and placements	43	30	8	19	536
Workshops	62	14	9	14	393
Administration	43	41	6	9	479
Other	51	20	10	19	505
Total (% of all)	(48)	(24)	(8)	(20)	5,565
Time on Scheme					
0–13 weeks	29	32	11	28	1,242
14–26 weeks	31	31	14	24	983
27–39 weeks	27	41	12	20	700
40 weeks or longer	68	14	3	15	2,667
Total (% of all)	(48)	(24)	(8)	(20)	5,592

custodial sentence), particularly if they lived in regions of above average unemployment. In the Midlands and the North a non-offender had as much chance of finding employment as an offender who lived in the South. Wales was unusual in that a comparatively high proportion of employees (offenders as well as non-offenders) went directly into a job. This may be because jobs were more likely to be found through informal methods, such as friends and relatives.

In a survey of schemes in mid-1986 most reported circulating job vacancies, giving assistance with the completion of application forms and supplying 'to whom it may concern' references. The majority also reported that they gave planned time off to visit local job centres and employment agencies. Just under half said they had arrangements for running courses on job-search or interview techniques, or issued information packs on these matters or on welfare benefit advice.

A follow-up survey of ex-participants in the local study areas was carried out at between six and twelve months after they had left the schemes. This found that, overall, less than a fifth had gone directly into a job on leaving their scheme. Most became unemployed. Six to twelve months later the position had not improved significantly, particularly in Areas NE and SL. In Area NE 13 per cent of those leaving the NACRO CP scheme were known to go to a job on leaving, and the percentage who had a job at the time of follow-up was the same. In Area SL there was very little change, from 12 per cent on leaving to 14 per cent on follow-up. In the other two local areas studied there were more marked improvements. Eleven per cent of those leaving the scheme in Area SW were known to go to jobs; six to twelve months later 21 per cent had jobs. In Area WM the improvement was from 16 per cent to 23 per cent. Approximately 5 per cent of ex-participants in each area were known to return to CP during the follow-up period. These analyses of the local areas indicate that, whatever the overall figures for the schemes when people leave, there were places where employment problems were both acute and persistent.

Summary

The NACRO CP schemes provided a range of work for people who were even more disadvantaged than other long-term unemployed adults in terms of their job prospects. There were, however, variations in what participants got from the schemes, depending on their sex, race, criminal history, and the area they came from. Most worked part time and remained, on average, for eight and a half months. Around half received some formal training in addition to what was learned whilst doing the job. Despite the disadvantages of the participants, the proportion going on to jobs on leaving was on a par with CP in general. However, there were areas where getting a job was especially difficult and there was evidence that jobs gained on leaving CP were often not sustained for long. Similarly, although the level of re-offending whilst known offenders were taking part in the schemes was at a modest level, suggesting a 'containment' effect, follow-up studies showed it was higher once people had left.

The value of the schemes

At one level both the YTS and the CP schemes achieved what they set out to do. Both programmes were delivered to a group of people of whom a high proportion had a background of educational and social disadvantage, including a criminal record. The schemes provided a range of work and training opportunities for those who took part in them. In addition to the formal requirements of the programmes the schemes took account of the special needs of participants by developing supportive relationships and by providing additional opportunities for participants to further their personal and vocational development. But there were also clearly limitations to what could be achieved through the schemes. Thus, the proportion of known offenders recruited to the CP schemes never achieved the level (70 per cent) that had initially been aimed at, and on YTS it was noticeable that the proportion of offenders, those without qualifications and with particular types of disadvantage, declined somewhat over time, especially as YTS moved towards the more demanding format of YTS 2.

Perhaps this is a matter of only limited significance since the programmes themselves were not specially intended to be schemes for offenders, even if they were being run by an agency concerned to ensure that offenders were given every opportunity to participate in them. Given that the schemes were intended to have a mixture of offenders and non-offenders, determining exactly what proportion should be offenders is a fairly arbitrary matter; especially because whether or not someone is a known offender is subject to an element of chance. On the other hand, it would clearly be a matter of interest and concern if the schemes demonstrably failed to appeal to offenders. It has already been suggested that the move to a more structured YTS programme was associated with a decline in the recruitment of less 'marketable' young people. It cannot be assumed that the link was causal, but if it were this would have implications for future programme planning. This is important because MSC programmes have tended to move along a path from a relatively loose format to a more highly structured arrangement. For young people the move has been from YOP, which permitted a great deal of variety, to the more formalized YTS 1, and eventually to the more demanding YTS 2, with each successive move denoting a shift away from a programme designed to respond to the needs of the unemployed and hard-to-employ, and towards the needs of employers.

On CP, although the formal structure remained much the same for some time, there were definite developments designed to move it from the 'responding to the unemployed' end of the spectrum, which included boosting the training element and certain areas of work, and involving employers more in the programme. This has since been taken even further with the incorporation of CP into a new Employment Training programme. Clearly care must be taken here not to suggest a crude and simplistic model. It is arguably desirable that the quality and content of programmes should be developed and improved. But perhaps what is important is the way that it is done, so that agencies and participants are permitted to develop their skills and expertise according to their background and experience. For many people on NACRO schemes, especially the young people who have had very unsettled lives and periods in institutions, simply gaining basic work habits and experience in a supportive environment is a considerable achievement. A rapid transformation into a skilled artificer or budding entrepreneur is in many, although not all, instances an unrealistic expectation. Form a sociological point of view it would be interesting to look at whether similar processes have occurred elsewhere during the early stages of the development of institutions. If so this might give grounds for the formulation of a theory of organizational progression which postulates that as institutions become more formalized, so they become more selective.

There were other differences between the two programmes studied. In terms of getting jobs and avoiding further court appearances, the participants on the NACRO CP schemes fared somewhat better than did those on the YTS schemes. As far as jobs were concerned, the NACRO CP schemes compared favourably with CP in general, whereas the proportion of those leaving the YTS schemes who got jobs was below YTS nationally. This may be because the proportion of offenders on the YTS schemes was higher than on the CP schemes and offenders were less likely to get jobs on leaving. The higher incidence of further court appearances amongst YTS trainees than CP workers is more problematic, but it is possible that the difference in age for the two programmes was an important factor, since re-offending tends to decline with age. In this context the discussion of age as a factor in the unemployment-crime link considered in Chapter 1 may be recalled. One cannot rule out the possibility that, because unemployment is a problem which affects the young more than others, it also has implications for the likelihood of their re-offending.

It is significant that participants with a serious history of offending did less well on the schemes than non-offenders and those with only a limited history of offending: they tended to leave earlier, to have done less whilst on the schemes, and to have poorer prospects when they left. This inevitably raises the issue of general versus special provision for the employment and training of offenders. In many ways it would be a backward step to resort to offender-only, sheltered work schemes and might not only perpetuate the identity of being an offender but also limit the opportunities and experience available to offenders. But within general programmes there should be recognition of the special needs of certain groups. Thus there is likely to be a continuing need for premium places on YTS and for a relaxation of eligibility and assessment criteria.

The potential for recruiting offenders to the schemes will also be affected by the attitude towards them of agencies such as the

Probation Service. As noted in Chapter 3 in the study of magistrates' courts, this attitude was often ambivalent. During the period of the research reported here the National Association of Probation Officers maintained a policy of opposition to government schemes like YTS and CP, and this may have had some influence on officers' preparedness to refer clients to them. Figures in this chapter have shown that the proportion of probation referrals to the schemes was both limited and declining, and many offenders who came to the schemes did so through other channels.

Apart from the differences between offenders and non-offenders on the schemes, the study demonstrated other important variations. There were differences between male and female and between white and black participants. These were apparent not so much in terms of access and recruitment as in how people experienced the schemes once on them. For example, whilst NACRO recruited a higher proportion of black people than the Programmes in general, there were indications that participation in the activities of the schemes varied between black and white people. These differences demonstrate that there is more to equality of opportunity than simply recruiting people. One also wonders whether recruiting a high proportion of black participants is necessarily to be regarded as an unmitigated achievement if it simply reflects the extent to which black people are discriminated against in the job market and were there because they could not get other work. Also relevant to equality of opportunity are the regional variations that were a consistent theme throughout the study: the finding that NACRO's employment and training schemes functioned differently in different parts of the country. Broadly speaking, schemes in the North recruited more convicted offenders than those in the South. But the range of work and training activities they provided was less extensive, and outcomes like getting a job were harder to achieve, even when differences in recruitment patterns were allowed for. Since these differences were evident at a regional level, they could not be explained simply as a matter of local idiosyncrasies in scheme management. Elements of inequality were therefore present within the network because of widely differing circumstances in different parts of the country.

If it is to succeed, each scheme needs to adapt to local social and economic conditions and take account of the interests of other agencies locally. But it then becomes important to ask at what point local variations cease to be desirable in order to facilitate flexible and effective operation, and become undesirable because of the inequalities of opportunity and outcome which they introduce. It is important to ask, also, what scope the provider may have to lessen those regional inequalities which already exist. Many of the variations were associated with different labour market conditions in the areas of operation. These clearly depended on forces which exerted a more powerful influence than anything NACRO could do to improve the operation of its schemes. During the winter of 1987, shortly after the research referred to here was completed, the 'North-South divide' became a phenomenon which attracted much popular and media attention. The terminology is too simplistic, but certainly pronounced regional variations were what the study had been recording for the previous three years. It is apparent that government schemes (and there is no reason to suppose that those run by NACRO are peculiar in this respect) fulfil very different functions in some parts of the country to those they fulfil in others. It may be all very well to think of YTS as 'a bridge between school and work' in the prosperous South-East; in some other places all too often it was a bridge between school and the dole queue. Broadly speaking, in the South schemes were able to gear themselves to training and enabling participants to take advantage of job opportunities. In the North and West they were largely geared to trying to manage the consequences of chronic unemployment. One such consequence was that offenders in those areas found it difficult to get on MSC schemes run by other sponsors who, unlike NACRO, were not so keen to take on offenders. This resulted in a higher proportion of offenders on the NACRO schemes in the North. The picture was more complicated than this, however, because there are areas with acute employment problems in the South as well. But the weight of evidence demonstrating the impact of external social and economic conditions on the schemes indicates the limitations to which such schemes are subject. And schemes themselves have only limited scope for changing such conditions. Certainly in the areas hardest hit by unemployment, their role was one of amelioration rather than transformation, and of helping communities to adjust to a deterioration in their economic and social circumstances.

What then of the longer term? What contribution can schemes make towards coping with the dual problems of unemployment and offending? This can probably be best summed up by saying it is an inevitably limited but vitally necessary one. NACRO chose to sponsor a network of employment and training schemes because this offered some opportunity for convicted offenders to make connections with the mainstream economy which they otherwise may not have had. But the structure of the economy has been undergoing a highly stressful process of change which has exposed many workers who are unskilled, or whose skills are redundant, to prolonged unemployment. This in turn has made the chances of disadvantaged groups making connections still more difficult. Increasingly, government sponsored programmes have been promoted as instruments for the creation of a more experienced, better skilled and more flexible workforce which will more readily fit the needs of employers. Yet for certain people and certain areas the programmes themselves may constitute the closest thing to the status of regular employment which they can expect to obtain. In economic terms, therefore, NACRO's experience as a voluntary organization venturing into employment and training schemes was that in the short run it was able to provide its recruits with more skills and experience in worthwhile work. But in the long run this had little effect on their position in local labour markets which already had surplus supplies of their skills. Thus these people remained on the margins of primary economic activity, and were left to move within what may be termed a secondary market for unskilled and surplus skill work which is supported at relatively low wage levels by government finance. Sponsoring work within this secondary market may therefore be seen as assisting in a process of supportive adjustment to the pressure of economic decline and restructuring, rather than as pushing forward new avenues of economic development or challenging the forces giving rise to economic stresses and strains.

In a simplistic model the schemes studied here might be seen as a means by which the unemployed get back into full employment and, if they are offenders, this might also be a step towards a crime-free life. If there are people who hold such naive expectations they are likely to be disappointed. A return to full-time employment is unlikely for many and for others employment patterns are likely to change, with more in the way of part-time and casual working (Handy 1984a). Government schemes are likely to play a residuary role in what has been termed a secondary labour market (Doeringer and Piore 1971). As has been seen, a proportion of participants had previously spent time on MSC schemes, and in various parts of the country the researchers observed that it was not uncommon for people to go on YTS, from there to CP or some other programme such as the Voluntary Projects Programme, perhaps doing a spot of casual work thereafter for a while or, more often, returning to the dole until they became eligible to rejoin CP. One American study has shown how illegitimate activity can become closely linked with legitimate activities in such a secondary labour market (Sviridoff and McElroy 1985: 5). The pessimistic scenario, therefore, is that we are seeing the re-emergence of what, in the USA, has been termed an underclass, and what in another era would have been called the lumpenproletariat, an accompanying feature of which is various economic survival strategies, both legitimate and illegitimate.

Is there a more optimistic scenario? One possibility is that instead of becoming temporary refuges for an underclass, government schemes could be vehicles for changing local economies by encouraging community enterprise initiatives. Such initiatives would, as far as possible, be identified with and belong to a particular locality. They would involve local people in delivering a range of socially useful services and products for their area. Such developments are badly needed to give the hope that employment and training schemes can open up possibilities, rather than be dead ends. If such initiatives were to succeed, however, they would need to be accompanied by policies which addressed the need to overcome regional inequalities, and to create more opportunities for employment and investment in the areas where they are needed most. In this context it is worth quoting the conclusions reached by Marris and Rein (1974: 126) in their study of employment programmes for offenders and other disadvantaged groups, undertaken 20 years ago but still relevant today:

> However resourceful the projects' employment programmes, they could do little to influence the economy which determined how many usable skills were in demand. ... In the last resort the success of the programmes depended upon the creation of jobs to use the young people they were trying to help ... they could only be provided by deliberate policy. ... Thus the projects could only achieve their aims within the framework of a national redistribution of resources, which deliberately redressed the balance of opportunities between rich and poor communities.

In the final chapter we consider further some of the issues referred to above.

Chapter six

Unemployed offenders and public policy

Past experience

In the preceding chapters we have presented a considerable amount of material relating to unemployment, crime, and offenders. It remains to draw this material together and consider its implications. This is not easy since it covers a wide range of issues. To start with the relationship between unemployment and crime was considered and it was concluded that unemployment is a factor which contributes to the incidence of crime, but in a way that is often complex and indirect, and is related to other factors. It is necessary to refer to particular offences and particular circumstances, rather than to unemployment and crime in general. We then went on to consider the impact of unemployment on the courts and sentencing, looking specifically at magistrates' courts. In contrast to earlier studies, which had mainly been based on the analysis of aggregate data, it was found that the impact of unemployment was more wide ranging than simply boosting the prison population. There was some relationship between employment status and the use of custody but, at least in the magistrates' courts studied, this was insufficiently strong to explain the extent of the association reported by previous research.

Furthermore the nature of the relationship was interesting: it was not so much a case of a more punitive attitude being displayed towards the unemployed as a concern to avoid the loss of a job for the employed, where possible. But equally important were the findings that unemployment has an effect throughout the sentencing range, influencing the use of fines, community service orders and, to some extent, probation. This presents courts and others with some difficult problems and restricts the options for all concerned. It was also found that courts' responses to unemployment varied in a way which reflected past sentencing practices and local social and economic conditions.

Finally, we looked at the value of employment and training

schemes for offenders. Here we found that such schemes have a range of objectives and that the expectations that different parties have of them can vary. They can successfully deliver a positive work and training experience to offenders and other people whose social disadvantages make it hard for them to compete in the labour market. The role played by schemes varies considerably, however, depending on the circumstances in which they operate. In particular, they were likely to have a harder task in the more economically deprived parts of the country, where their role was often one of assuaging the impact of deprivation. In more affluent areas, on the other hand, it was possible for them to operate in terms of skill training and preparation for work. Thus, although the schemes were running well, their ability to influence the availability of jobs and the level of crime was limited. The conclusion was that employment and training schemes have a part to play in resettling and sustaining offenders in the community, but that their ability to do so depends on the social and economic conditions prevailing in the wider society.

Is there a thread that links these different issues – crime, the courts, and employment schemes – apart from the fact that they are all concerned with unemployment and with offenders? There would be a certain sense of completeness in being able to recount that unemployment leads to crime, that in the ensuing court cases the unemployed are dealt with more harshly, many of them going to prison, that this reinforces the cycle of joblessness and crime, but that a knight on a white charger is at hand in the shape of employment and training schemes to rescue the offenders and set them back on the road to a productive and law-abiding life. Such a story line would have something of the appeal of a Victorian novel, with virtue triumphing over adversity. And it has to be said that, although a caricature, there is an element of truth in each stage of this 'Offender's Progress'. There is some evidence to support particular bits of it, as well as to support the contention that a vicious cycle of disadvantage and offending can occur if nothing is done. But the story is complicated by the fact that at all stages there are qualifications and an interplay of different factors. A crude determinist model will not suffice. The nature of any relationship between unemployment and crime depends on whom one is referring to, what crimes are involved, how they are dealt with, and the broader social conditions in an area as well as the nature of its employment problems. Similarly the sentencing of offenders involves many considerations, with a person's employment status and history featuring in only a secondary role. The impact of employment and training schemes, too, depends very much on the conditions in which they have to operate, the varying perceptions of their role, and the fact that they are developed in the context of economic and employment policy, with little recognition of their significance for criminal justice policy.

The corollary of this is that since there are no simple explanations, there will be no simple solutions. In recent years the focus of criminal justice policy has shifted from the treatment of offenders to the prevention or, more accurately, reduction of crime. However, crime reduction can take different forms, one of which might include social measures like employment schemes. There is a case for mounting a study to test the value of such an approach. Meanwhile, research into methods of crime prevention suggests that there are no universal remedies there either; that what is needed is careful analysis of particular situations so that any form of intervention suits local conditions (Winchester and Jackson 1982). This means that people concerned with crime prevention need to be aware of, amongst other things, the local social and economic environment and how it may affect the incidence of crime. It means that individual courts should examine their practices in the light of employment conditions in the communities they serve, and it means that those who establish employment and training schemes for offenders should do so in the full knowledge of what the likely prospects are given the nature of both unemployment and the crime problem in their area. The response to unemployment, crime, and offenders cannot stop there, however. If it did, this would simply serve to perpetuate the regional inequalities that have been noted. There must also be regional and national policies designed to ensure that resources are directed where they are needed and not left to the vagaries of market forces.

Future prospects

As with much research this book has looked backwards and reported what is now past. From what has been found, is it possible to look forwards and see what lessons there might be for the future? To some extent this depends on what the future holds, and in particular on future levels of unemployment. In 1985 the Director of Special Measures of the Manpower Services Commission predicted that, 'in 1990 we will have an even greater unemployment problem than the one which faces us today' and 'there will be a persistent problem of unemployment throughout the next decade' (Surr 1985). In 1987 a study by the Institute for Employment Research (1987) forecast that, even with growth in the economy regaining pre-1973 levels, unemployment would only come down to 2.8 million by 1990 and 2.5 million by 1995. Furthermore, many more jobs would be part time and in sectors of the labour market requiring skills and professional training. On the other hand 1987 saw some decline in the official figures for those unemployed and claiming benefit. But the next year a report by an MSC Special Working Group on unemployment expressed concern at the continuing high number of long-term unemployed: 'The danger is that this large group of people will be left stranded: unable, because of prolonged inactivity and the lack of appropriate skills to compete for jobs as they become available' (MSC 1988: para. 1). Speculation on possible future levels of unemployment is difficult as these can be affected by world trade markets and the likelihood of recession, as well as by changes in government policy. The problem of trying to predict what level unemployment will reach in the future reinforces the need to address specific areas of concern, including the needs of particular groups such as offenders.

Whatever the level of unemployment, the need to deal with unemployed offenders does not disappear; it only changes. As pointed out in an earlier chapter, unemployment is still a problem as far as offenders are concerned, even at times when unemployment nationally is low. As one study has rather bluntly suggested, 'Those groups ... who are most prone to commit the kind of crimes considered here (violent and property crime) may not participate in the labour force to any significant degree regardless of the general state of the economy' (Parker and Horwitz 1986: 169). Clearly low unemployment is preferable to high unemployment, but whether unemployment is low or high, offenders are going to need special help in gaining access to jobs and training. Unless that help is available, offenders are likely to form part of an underclass, who remain marginal to the sphere of legitimate economic activity. Given that the relationship between unemployment and crime is such a variable and conditional one, it is difficult to estimate what impact unemployment is likely to have on the nature and extent of crime for the rest of this century. But clearly measures designed to tackle crime in a particular locality should not ignore the employment situation there. This has become increasingly apparent in the concern about what are generally referred to as the 'inner cities', where even a government that denies any link between unemployment and crime tacitly acknowledges that jobs are a major part of the problem in such areas.

On the other hand, since other factors besides unemployment can affect the incidence of crime, it is possible that ways may be found of managing the crime problem even with a high level of unemployment. The perception of unemployment as a problem may diminish. In the early 1980s unemployment reached a level unprecedented in the post-war era and unthinkable a decade before. It is arguable that society has adjusted, and will continue to adjust, to higher levels of unemployment than previously. This could be interpreted as meaning that those in society who have jobs are happy to ignore those who do not; whether the victims of unemployment will adjust is more doubtful. They may come to 'accept their lot', or the 'have nots' may become even more desperate to gain illegitimately what the 'haves' can gain by legitimate means. In this context it is worth noting that the age group of unemployed people to whom, from 1988, the government seeks to apply pressure to join training schemes, by withdrawing benefit from those who refuse, is the same as the age group – 16 to 25 – who are responsible for most crime.

The role of employment and training schemes

Jobs have been seen by the government as coming from the development of new enterprise. The role of employment and training schemes has been seen as both helping to build that enterprise and to take advantage of the job opportunities it offers. This means a better-trained and more skilled workforce. But in the climate that has developed in the 1980s, it also means a workforce prepared to undertake work on a different basis than previously. For many people this is likely to mean more part-time and short-term work, with less job security, less health and safety safeguards (Box 1987: 55–60) and less pay at the bottom end of the market. Does this mean, as suggested earlier, that those with criminal convictions will miss out on job opportunities and form part of a new underclass, just as they formed part of the old lumpenproletariat? Organizations like NACRO, Apex and the Probation Services have tried to prevent this happening by seeking to ensure that offenders do not miss whatever is available. But both statutory and non-statutory services have found themselves in something of a cleft stick. Probation Services have, on the one hand sought to respond to their clients' needs for employment, whilst on the other trying to come to terms with the need to help people cope with unemployment (Walton 1987). Similarly the NACRO employment and training schemes in the South of the country were more likely to be able to address participants' needs for employment by helping to prepare them for jobs, whereas in the North they trained them in survival skills. So it is important to have realistic expectations about what can be achieved.

In recent years much emphasis has been placed on performance measures and similar instruments of good management. However desirable these may be in themselves, they are no guarantee that the intended outcome will be achieved. Dealing with a problem depends as much on having made a correct analysis of the problem and an appropriate response to it as on how well managed the response is. Thus, an employment scheme can be well run, but still be the wrong kind of scheme for the purpose, be under-resourced, or be struggling against forces beyond its control. The evidence for the NACRO YTS and CP schemes was that they were well managed and doing what they were supposed to do. But they were not always able to provide the jobs for people to go to afterwards. Much depends on how the problem is defined in the first place. If the problem of unemployment is seen as stemming from shortcomings in the workforce, then schemes should be developed which remedy these according to the capacities of the individual participants. If, on the other hand the problem is a shortage of jobs then steps need to be taken to stimulate the economy. Of course it is possible that an element of both is needed. During the 1980s the government presented unemployment as being a consequence of a lack of enterprise and a lack of skills in the workforce. The result has been a radical transformation of training for work. It may be that a better trained workforce does have some effect on jobs. But if the government's thesis is flawed, and the problem is a shortage of jobs rather than, or as well as, the shortcomings of people, then no amount of training can make up for the lack of job opportunities. Though the size of the so-called 'black economy' is unknown, among its participants are likely to be people who, lacking alternative employment, find other ways of surviving. Is the black economy therefore to be regarded as a safety valve or a threat to more legitimate forms of employment?

The changing nature of work means that in future more people than previously are likely to experience periods without employment and will need training. Handy (1984b) and Atkinson (1984) describe how the old employment pattern of corporations being staffed by a stable, permanent full-time workforce has been giving way to one in which firms have a small core of career employees surrounded by a larger periphery of people whose skills and labour are brought in from time to time in accordance with the fluctuating demands of business. This means that, for many people, in future work will be on a contractual, short-term or part-time basis. Adaptable workers and transferable skills will be demanded and more people than previously are likely to experience periods without employment when they will need further training. In such a context employment and training schemes will continue to be necessary and may indeed become more widespread as a means whereby workers gain new skills. Schemes will need to be well-planned, adequately resourced, and produced in consultation with all those who have an interest in their success. They should take account of all ranges of need and ability and be administered on a basis which ensures that they are an integral part of the community they serve. They should, in other words, pursue true equality of opportunity, and this will involve providing for people with convictions and those without. The role of agencies like NACRO and the Probation Service will be to ensure that offenders are not left to 'scuffle round the edges' (Handy 1984a: 23).

In some ways work with unemployed offenders can be said to have benefited from the range of measures that have been developed in response to large scale unemployment. Chapter 4 recounted how employment and training schemes for offenders were at first small-scale special projects, and how they grew and became aligned with general provision for the unemployed. How should they proceed in future? We have seen that as YTS moved to a more formal and demanding structure the proportion of offenders recruited to the NACRO YTS schemes declined somewhat. This may be different when YTS refusers are denied benefit, but it highlights the question (referred to in Chapter 5) of whether the most socially disadvantaged people, including offenders, should be catered for by special schemes tailored to their needs, or by general provision. We believe the answer lies with general schemes, but they need to be the right kind of schemes. Beyond this, the success of the schemes will depend on the extent to which the availability of work is perceived as a skills deficiency or a jobs deficiency. Failure to match the supply of training by a supply of jobs will increase disillusionment, and disillusionment can easily result in disaffection and a resort to other, less legitimate, means of pursuing material and personal satisfaction.

The role of justice

What then of criminal justice and penal policy? This has tended to go its own way in the past, paying little heed to other areas of social policy. This is probably because it has traditionally regarded itself, and hence been regarded by others, as not like other policy areas; as somewhat apart from, if not above, the rest. Such a perception has been reinforced by the relatively favoured position of the 'law and order' budget in recent years. It is not certain, however, that either the budget or the policies can be so insulated in future. Like it or not, the research presented in this book shows that unemployment does have an effect on the courts and associated agencies. This has to be seen in the context of the historical links between work and the law referred to in Chapter 2. The time has come for a re-appraisal of measures for dealing with offenders which are in some way linked with assumptions about work and income. Criminal justice cannot be entirely divorced from social justice.

One matter that has not been considered here is work and training in Prison Department establishments. This is a subject which deserves greater attention than it has received hitherto. Whilst there have been limited attempts to develop initiatives in prisons to equip offenders for worthwhile jobs on their release (e.g. at Coldingley), by and large the history of work and employment in prisons has been a dismal one. The Prison Service Industries and Farms organization has not been a notable success thus far (Stern 1987: 145) and the principal activity in many prisons is that of being confined to one's cell for many hours a day. On release the arrangements for linking ex-prisoners to employment and training opportunities, whether on schemes or the open market, have been limited. There have been the schemes run by Apex and NACRO, but establishing the eligibility of ex-prisoners to gain access to YTS and CP schemes has been an uphill struggle. Some prisoners do have the means to find their own way back to work. A study of a northern prison found that many of the discharged prisoners who found work did so through their own family and community networks rather than through the activities of any agency (Corden *et al.* 1978). There is the potential for much greater co-ordination between community-based employment and training provision and that which takes place in prison. This could be greatly enhanced if prisoners were more often able to serve their sentences in prisons close to their homes and the communities to which they will return on their release. Given that ex-prisoners find it harder to go straight into jobs on release if unemployment is high, they should at least be assured of ease of access to training provision, both whilst inside and on release. For young offenders perhaps more could be done to increase the compatibility of YTS training and that found in Youth Custody Centres. There have been some moves in this direction in at least one Centre (Home Office 1985b: para. 217), and further research is being undertaken on this during 1987–8 by the NACRO Research Unit. With further developments in adult training, perhaps training in prisons could share a 'common core' of subjects with outside programmes.

The question was posed earlier as to whether there was a central theme linking the matters considered in this book. We believe there is. We believe that thread is the importance of making it possible for offenders, and those at risk of offending, to have a stake in society which is not dependent on law-breaking. Since 'society' is too unwieldy and abstract a concept for many practical purposes, this amounts to saying a stake in whatever communities they are part of or can identify with. Under the traditional work ethic a job has had this function to a large extent. As a consequence courts tended to regard a job and a steady work history as evidence that the offender retained a commitment to 'respectable' society and made a contribution to it. Magistrates' courts, at least, now seek to preserve this when they can by trying to avoid sending the employed to prison. But with the changing patterns of work, whether these involve different skills, more part-time and temporary work, or no work, the concept of the individual's stake in society must be seen in broader terms. Greater emphasis should be placed on activities other than gainful employment which contribute to the common good such as good parenting, care of elderly and disabled relatives, and involvement in community activities like tenants' associations. As far as training schemes are concerned, more attention needs to be paid to local job markets and the work of employment schemes should be related to the needs of local communities. Hence initiatives need to be locally based, but within a framework of national resources and planning.

People taking part in employment and training schemes should, as a consequence, be encouraged to consider their communities' needs and take an active part in responding to them. So the 'training for life' offered to participants would include not just individual survival skills, like cooking, budgeting, and education for leisure, but discussions on the local economy, information about local resources and agencies, and how to develop local services and enterprises. The magistrates' court is also a local institution and we found magistrates were very concerned about the future of the communities they serve and, in particular, about the future for young people growing up without the prospect of work. However, more could be done to inform magistrates about, and involve them in, the work of employment and training schemes in their area. As influential citizens magistrates can help to promote ideas for improving local services. Enabling offenders to develop a stake in the communities in which they live might help prevent the development of a criminal underclass. But it requires the support of individuals, public and private investment and, above all, government policies designed to overcome inequalities and promote social, as well as criminal, justice.

To date official reaction to unemployment among offenders has tended to be minimal and *ad hoc*, seeing such social and economic matters as marginal to criminal justice. But there has also been another kind of reaction, which has received official sanction. The 1980s have been characterized not only by high unemployment and high crime, but by a resurgence of what is usually termed the 'law and order' response to crime, with calls for 'tougher' action against those offenders who are caught and convicted; calls which have evoked favourable responses from the government in the form of more powers for the courts, a greater use of custodial sentences, an increase in the severity of some regimes, and restrictions on the use of parole. We are reminded of the prophetic remarks of a 1976 UN report, that the impact of economic recession is likely to be reflected not only in more crime but in 'a more massive and costly repression machinery in an attempt to control the crime' (UNSDRI 1976: 16). Historically this is not surprising since societal instability and the uncertainties it engenders have been observed in the past to provoke repressive actions against sections of the community who become the scapegoats for society's ills (Fromm 1960). However, we would want to end by arguing that, in a modern society, economic recession and unemployment should be accompanied by a constructive rather than a repressive response to the majority of crime and criminals. Whilst unemployment cannot excuse particular acts of law-breaking, simply getting tough with offenders and building more prisons is not the solution, and may well make matters worse by increasing the chances of further offending. The ways that offenders are dealt with in the courts and in the community may not provide the whole answer to crime, but they are an important element in the strategy needed to deal with it. This strategy should be looking to ways of strengthening community structures at a time when such structures are under considerable pressure. How to give offenders the opportunity to play a constructive part in that task is the challenge that faces us all.

Appendix one

Further information on the magistrates' courts

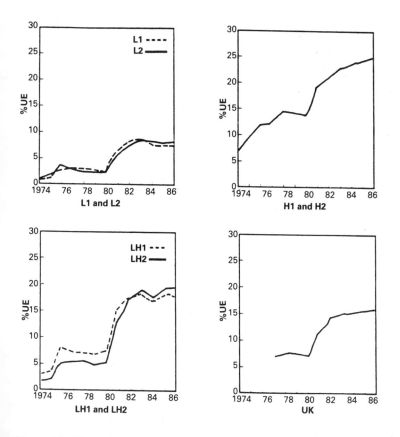

Figure A1 Unemployment rates for the six courts and for the UK
Source: Employment Gazette

Appendix

Unemployment rates

Figure A1 shows the unemployment rates in the 'travel to work areas' served by the six courts and in the UK, as at February each year. H1 and H2 were in the same area. The contrast between the L, H, and LH rates satisfies the requirements of the research design.

Custody rates

Figure A2 shows each court's proportionate use of custodial sentences (including suspended sentence and committed for sentence) for males aged 17–20, and 21+, found guilty of indictable offences.

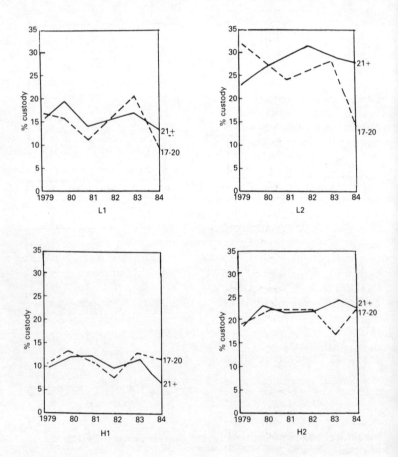

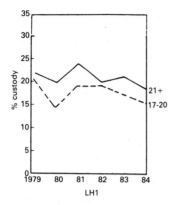
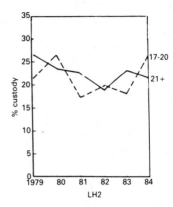

Figure A2 Custodial sentencing rates at the six courts
Source: Home Office Statistics

The contrasts in the L and H courts accord with the research design. The LH courts, though having fairly similar rates for all custodial sentences together, differed in other ways, especially their use of discharges and community service orders.

The records samples

Table A1 shows the percentages of men unemployed, and of men sentenced to immediate custody, in the records samples studied at the six courts. The L courts contrasted with the H and LH courts in unemployment rates, and L1, H1, and LH1 contrasted with L2, H2, and LH2 in the use of custody; thus the samples fitted the research design.

Table A1 Records samples: unemployment and custody rates

Crown	L1	L2	H1	H2	LH1	LH2
% Unemployed	46	45	65	71	71	67
% sentenced to detention centre, youth custody, immediate imprisonment or committed to Crown Court for sentence	9	17	8	16	11	20
N (100%)	553	517	664	585	599	582

References

Ashworth, A., Genders, E., Mansfield, G., Peay, J. and Player, E. (1984) *Sentencing in the Crown Court: Report of an Exploratory Study*, Occasional Paper no. 10, University of Oxford: Centre for Criminological Research.

Atkinson, J. (1984) 'Manpower strategies for flexible organisations', *Personnel Management*, August: 28–31.

Banks, C. and Fàirhead, S. (1976) *The Petty Short-Term Prisoner*, Chichester: Barry Rose.

Beeson, M. (1965) 'Juvenile delinquency, unemployment and the probation officer', PhD. thesis, University of Durham.

Belson, W. A. (1968) 'The extent of stealing by London boys and some of its origins', *The Advancement of Science*, 25 (124): 1–15.

Boshier, R. and Johnson, D. (1974) 'Does conviction affect employment opportunities?', *British Journal of Criminology*, 14 (3): 264–8.

Box, S. and Hale, C. (1982) 'Economic crisis and the rising prisoner population in England and Wales', *Crime and Social Justice,* 17: 20–35.

Box, S. (1987) *Recession, Crime and Punishment*, London: Macmillan.

Brenner, M. H. (1976a) *Estimating the Social Cost of National Economic Policy: Implications for Mental and Physical Health and Criminal Aggression*, Joint Economic Committee, Congress of the United States, US Govt. Printing Office, Washington.

—— (1976b) 'Time series analysis – effects of the economy on criminal behaviour and the administration of criminal justice' (analysis of data from the United States, Canada, England, Wales, and Scotland) in United Nations Social Defence Research Institute, *Economic Crises and Crime*, Rome.

Brody, S. (1976) *The Effectiveness of Sentencing: a review of the literature*, Home Office Research Study no. 35, London: HMSO.

Buikhuisen, W. and Hoekstra, H. A. (1974) 'Factors related to recidivism', *British Journal of Criminology* 14 (1): 63–9.

Casale, S. S. G. and Hillsman, S. T. (1986) *The Enforcement of Fines as Criminal Sanctions: the English Experience and its Relevance to American Practice, (Executive Summary)*, London and New York: Vera Institute of Justice.

Centre for Econometric Studies of the Justice System (1979) *A Review of*

Some of the Results in Estimating the Social Cost of National Economic Policy: implications for mental and physical health and criminal aggression, Hoover Institution.

Chandler, D. (1987) *Fine Enforcement: ideas from a survey*, Institute of Criminology Occasional Paper No. 15, University of Cambridge, Cambridge.

Collins, J. J. (ed.) (1982) *Drinking and Crime*, London, Tavistock.

Convery, P. (1987) 'How many unemployed are there?' *Initiatives* 4 (3): 3–6

Corden, J. (1976) 'Prisoners' rights and National Insurance contribution and benefits', *The Howard Journal of Criminal Justice* XV (2): 13–30.

—— Kuipers, J. and Wilson, K. (1978) *After Prison: a study of the post-release experiences of discharged prisoners*, University of York.

Crow, I. D. and Richardson, P. (1985) *Youth Training and Young Offenders*, Research and Development Report no. 24, MSC.

—— and Simon, F. H. (1987) *Unemployment and Magistrates' Courts*, London: NACRO.

Davies, M. (1969) *Probationers in their Social Environment*, Home Office Research Study no. 2, London: HMSO.

—— (1974) *Prisoners of Society: attitudes and after-care*, London and Boston: Routledge and Kegan Paul.

Deakin, B. M. and Pratten, C. F. (1987) 'Economic effects of YTS', *Employment Gazette,* vol. 95, no. 10: 491–7.

Department of Education and Science and Others (1985) *Education and Training for Young People* (White Paper) Cmnd. 9482, HMSO.

Department of Employment (1981) *A New Training Initiative: A Programme for Action* (White Paper) Cmnd. 8455, London: HMSO.

—— (1984) *Training for Jobs* (White Paper) Cmnd. 9135, London: HMSO.

—— (1985) 'A survey of Youth Training Scheme providers', *Employment Gazette*, 93 (8): 307–12.

—— (1986) *Labour Force Survey 1985*, London.

—— (1987) *Employment Gazette* 95, 12, Table 2.6.

Digby, P. W. (1976) *Hostels and Lodgings for Single People*, OPCS. London: HMSO.

Doeringer, P. B. and Piore, M. J. (1971) *Internal Labour Markets and Manpower Analysis*, Lexington, Massachusetts: D. C. Heath.

Engels, F. (1969) *Condition of the Working Class in England*, London: Panther.

Evans, R. (1968) 'The labour market and parole success', *Journal of Human Resources*, 3 (2): 201–12.

Ewing, B. G. (1977) 'Unemployment and crime: are they bedfellows?' Testimony before Subcommittee on Crime of the House of Representatives Committee on the Judiciary, in *LEAA Newsletter*, 6 (16): 2.

Farrington, D. P., Gallagher, B., Morley, L., St Ledger, R. J. and West, D. J. (1986) 'Unemployment, school leaving and crime', *British Journal of Criminology*, 26 (4): 335–56.

—— and Morris, A. M. (1983) 'Sex, sentencing and reconviction', *British Journal of Criminology*, 23 (3): 229–48.

References

Field, S. and Southgate, P. (1982) *Public Disorder*, Home Office Research Study no. 72, London: HMSO.

Fleisher, B. M. (1963) 'The effect of unemployment on juvenile delinquency', *Journal of Political Economy*, 71: 543–55.

—— (1969) 'The effect of income on delinquency', *Economic Review*, 56 (1).

Fromm, E. (1960) *Fear of Freedom*, London: Routledge.

Fry, T. and Gill, L. (1988) *A Logit Analysis of Sentencing Data from Magistrates Courts in England and Wales*, University of Manchester.

Gibbs, J. P. (1966) 'Crime, unemployment and status integration', *British Journal of Criminology*, 6 (1): 49–58.

Gladstone, F. (1979) 'Crime and the crystal ball', *Home Office Research Unit Bulletin No. 7*. London: Home Office.

Glaser, D. and Rice, K. (1959) 'Crime, age and employment', *American Sociological Review*, 24: 679–86.

Gormally, B., Lyner, O., Mulligan, G. and Warden, M. (1981) *Unemployment and Young Offenders in Northern Ireland,* Belfast: NIACRO.

Gravelle, H. S. E., Hutchinson, G. and Stern, J. (1981) *Mortality and Unemployment: A Cautionary Note*. Discussion Paper No. 95. Centre for Labour Economics, London School of Economics.

Greater Manchester Probation Service (1986) *Employment Matters*, Report of a Working Group, Greater Manchester Probation Service.

Greenberg, D. F. (1977) 'The dynamics of oscillatory punishment processes', *Journal of Criminal Law and Criminology*, 68: 643–51.

Handy, C. (1984a) *The Future of Work*, London: Penguin.

—— (1984b) 'The organisation revolution and how to harness it', *Personnel Management*, July: 18–23.

Harding, J. (1978) *Employment and the Probation and After-Care Service*, NACRO Chichester: Barry Rose.

—— (ed.) (1987) *Probation and the Community: a practice and policy reader*, London: Tavistock.

Harraway, P. C., Brown, A. J., Hignett, C. F., Wilson, C. O., Abbot, J. S., Mortimer, S. A. and Keegan, A. C. (1985) *The Demonstration Unit, 1981–1985*, Inner London Probation Service.

Hawkins, K. (1984) *Unemployment*, London: Penguin.

Henry, A. F. and Short, J. F. (1954) *Suicide and Homicide*, Glencoe: Illinois Press.

HMSO (1985) *Employment: the Challenge for the Nation*, Cmnd. 9474, London: HMSO.

Home Office (1963) *The Organisation of After-Care*, Report of the Advisory Council on the Treatment of Offenders, London: HMSO.

—— (1970) *Non-Custodial and Semi-Custodial Penalties*, Report of the Advisory Council on the Penal System, London: HMSO.

—— (1974) *Working Party on Vagrancy and Street Offences Working Paper*, Appendix A, London: HMSO.

—— (1978) 'A survey of the south east prison population', *Research Bulletin no. 5*, pp. 12–24, Home Office Research Unit.

—— (1984a) *Criminal Statistics, England and Wales*, London: HMSO.

—— (1984b) *Prison Statistics, England and Wales*, London: HMSO.

—— (1985a) 'Criminal careers of people born in 1953, 1958 and 1963', *Statistical Bulletin*, 7/85, Home Office.

—— (1985b) *Report on the Work of the Prison Department, 1984/85* Cmnd. 9699, London: HMSO.

Hood, R. (1972) *Sentencing the Motoring Offender*, Cambridge Studies in Criminology, London: Heinemann.

House of Commons Official Report (1986) 'Written answers', 13 Jan., col. 457.

Ignatieff, M. (1978) *A Just Measure of Pain*, London: Macmillan.

Institute for Employment Research (1987) *Review of the Economy and Unemployment 1987*, University of Warwick.

Jankovic, I. (1977) 'Labour market and imprisonment', *Crime and Social Justice*, 9: 17–31.

Jardine, E., Moore, G. and Pease, K. (1983) 'Community Service Orders, employment and the tariff', *Criminal Law Review*, 17–20.

Justice of the Peace (1982a) 'Unemployment and crime', *Justice of the Peace*, p. 684.

—— (1982b) 'A job to go to Monday, notes of the week', *Justice of the Peace*, p. 700.

Lowson, D. (1970) *City Lads in Borstal*, Liverpool University Press.

McLintock, F. H. (1976) 'The Beeson Report: delinquency and unemployment in the North-East of England', in *Economic Crises and Crime*, UNSDRI: Rome.

Magistrates' Courts Act (1980) London: HMSO.

Mannheim, H. (1940) 'Crime and unemployment', in *Social Aspects of Crime in England between the Wars*, London: Allen and Unwin. (Reprinted in, Carson, W. G. and Wiles, P. (eds) (1971) *Crime and Delinquency in Britain*, London: Martin Robertson.

Manpower Services Commission (1976) *Action Research Programme for Disadvantaged People*, Sheffield: MSC.

—— (1977) *New Special Programmes for the Unemployed*, Sheffield: MSC.

—— (1981a) *A New Training Initiative*, Sheffield: MSC.

—— (1981b) *A New Training Initiative: An Agenda for Action*, Sheffield: MSC.

—— (1982) *Youth Task Group Report*, Sheffield: MSC.

—— (1983a) *Towards an Adult Training Strategy*, Sheffield: MSC.

—— (1983b) *Corporate Plan, 1983–84*, Sheffield: MSC.

—— (1983c) *Equal Opportunities in the Youth Training Scheme for Young Ex-Offenders*, YTB/83/5, Sheffield: MSC.

—— (1984a) *Annual Report, 1983/84*, Sheffield: MSC.

—— (1984b) *A New Training Initiative: Modernisation of Occupational Training*, Sheffield: MSC.

—— (1984c) *A Handbook for Community Projects*, Sheffield: MSC.

—— (1986) *100% Follow-Up of YTS Leavers*, Sheffield: MSC, YTB/86/N12.

—— (1988) *Towards a New Adult Training Programme*, Sheffield: MSC/88/1.

Marris, P. and Rein, M. (1974) *Dilemmas of Social Reform*, London: Pelican.

Marshall, T. F., Fairhead, S. M., Murphy, D. J. I. and Iles, S. C. (1978) 'Evaluation for democracy', in *Seminar for Social Research in the Public Sector*, ESOMAR, Heidelberg, Fed. Rep. of Germany, 41–61.

Martin, J. P. (1962) *Offenders as Employees*, London: Macmillan.

—— and Webster, W. (1971) *Social Consequences of Conviction*, London: Heinemann.

Martinson, R. (1974) 'What works? Questions and answers about prison reform', *The Public Interest*, 35: 22–54.

—— (1979) 'New findings, new views: a note of caution regarding sentencing reform', *Hofstra Law Review*, 7 (2).

Mays, J. B. (1963) *Crime and the Social Structure*, London: Faber.

Maxwell, J. (1969) *Sixteen Years On: a follow-up of the 1947 Scottish survey*, University of London Press.

Millar, A. R. (1984) *The Experimental Introduction of Fines Enforcement Officers into Two Sheriff Courts*, Central Research Unit, Scottish Office.

Morris, P. and Beverley, F. (1975) *On Licence: A Study of Parole*, London: Wiley.

Moxon, D. (1983) 'Fine default, unemployment and the use of imprisonment', *Home Office Research Bulletin no. 16*, Home Office.

NACRO (1977) *NACRO's Response to MSC document 'New Special Programmes for the Unemployed – the Next Steps'*, London: NACRO.

—— (1978) *Youth Opportunities Programme: Application to Area Board of the MSC*, London: NACRO.

—— (1979) *An Employment Project for Young People at Risk*, London: NACRO.

—— (1981a) *Fine Default: Report of a NACRO Working Party*, London: NACRO.

—— (1981b) *Response to the Manpower Service Commission's Consultative Document, 'A New Training Initiative'*, London: NACRO.

—— (1981c) *Towards the New Training Initiative: A Proposal to the Manpower Services Commission*, London: NACRO.

—— (1982) *NACRO Statement of Policy on CP*, London: NACRO.

—— (1983a) *NACRO and the CP: Background Paper for Staff*, London: NACRO.

—— (1983b) *Access to YTS for Young Ex-Offenders*, NACRO Employment Advisory Committee Paper 9/83.

—— (1983c) *Unemployment, Training and Resettling Ex-Offenders: A Response to, 'Towards an Adult Training Strategy'*, London: NACRO.

—— (1983d) *Learning the Job: A Paper for Discussion with the Manpower Services Commission*, London: NACRO.

—— (1984) *Submission to the House of Commons Employment Committee on the Effects of the Shift in Provision from Mode B places Towards Employer-led Work-Based Mode A Places*, London: NACRO.

National Youth Bureau (1981) *Community Involvement by Young People:*

An Area Survey, Young Volunteer Resources Unit, National Youth Bureau.

Norrington, D., Brodie, H. and Munro, J. (1986) *Value for Money in the Community Programme*, Department of Employment/Manpower Services Commission.

Northumbria Police (1979, 1980) *Annual Report of the Chief Constable*.

Nott, D. and Corden, J. (1980) *Deferment of Sentence by Courts in West Yorkshire*, Department of Social Administration and Social Work, University of York.

Ogburn, W. F. and Thomas, D. S. (1922) 'The influence of the business cycle on certain social conditions', *Journal of the American Statistical Association*, XVII: 305-40.

Parker, H. (1986) *Drug Misuse in Wirral*, University of Liverpool.

——, Newcombe, R. and Bakx, K. (1986) *Heroin and Crime*, University of Liverpool.

Parker, R. N. and Horwitz, A. V. (1986) 'Unemployment, crime, and Imprisonment: A Panel Approach', *Criminology*, 24 (4): 751-73.

Pease, K. (1980) *Prison Populations*, Milton Keynes: Open University Press.

Phillips, L., Votey, H. L. and Maxwell, D. (1972) 'Crime, youth and the labour market: an econometric study', *Journal of Political Economy*, 80: 491-504.

Phillpotts, G. J. O. and Lancucki, L. B. (1979) *Previous Convictions, Sentence and Reconviction*, Home Office Research Study no. 53, London: HMSO.

Quinney, R. (1977) *Class, State and Crime*, Longman: New York.

Richman, J. and Draycott, A. T. (1984) *Stone's Justices' Manual*, London: Butterworth.

Rossi, P. M., Berk, R. A. and Lenihan, K. J. (1980) *Money, Work and Crime: Experimental Evidence*, London: Academic Press.

Rutter, M. and Madge, N. (1976) *Cycles of Disadvantage* (Ch. 6, Crime and Delinquency), London: Heinemann.

Samuels, A. (1982) 'Sentencing the unemployed offender', *Justice of the Peace*, 643-4.

Showler, B. and Sinfield, A. (eds) (1981) *The Workless State*, Oxford: Martin Robertson.

Silberman, M. and Chapman, B. (1971) 'After-care units in London, Liverpool and Manchester', in *Explorations in After-Care*, Home Office Research Unit Study no. 9, HMSO.

Smith, D. J. (1983) *Police and People in London, Volume I: A Survey of Londoners*, London: Policy Studies Institute.

Softley, P. (1978) *Fines in Magistrates' Courts*, Home Office Research Study no. 46, HMSO.

—— (1983) 'The imprisonment of fine defaulters', *Justice of the Peace*, 470-2.

Soothill, K. (1974) *The Prisoner's Release: a study of the employment of ex-prisoners*, London: Allen & Unwin.

Stern, V. (1987) *Bricks of Shame*, London: Penguin.

Stinchcombe, A. L. (1963) 'Institutions of privacy in the determination of police administrative practice', *American Journal of Sociology*, 69 (2).

Surr, J. (1985) 'The changing patterns of employment', in, *Idle Hands*, London: Apex, BIC, NACRO.

Sviridoff, M. and McElroy, J. (1985) *Employment and Crime: A Summary Report*, London and New York: Vera Institute of Justice.

Taggart, R. (1972) *The Prison of Unemployment*, Baltimore: Johns Hopkins University Press.

Tarling, R. (1982) 'Unemployment and crime', *Research Bulletin no. 14*, Home Office Research and Planning Unit.

—— and Weatheritt, M. (1979) *Sentencing Practice in Magistrates' Courts*, Home Office Research Study no. 56, London: HMSO.

Thornton, D. (1987) 'Treatment effects on recidivism: a reappraisal of the "Nothing Works" doctrine', in, McGurk, B. J., Thornton, D. and Williams, M. (eds) *Applying Psychology to Imprisonment: theory and practice*, London: HMSO.

—— Curran, L., Grayson, D. and Holloway, J. (1984) *Tougher Regimes in Detention Centres: report of an evaluation by the young offender psychology unit*, London: HMSO.

Thorpe, J. (1978) *Social Enquiry Reports: a survey*, Home Office Research Study no. 48, London: HMSO.

Tidmarsh, D., Wood, S. and King, J. K. (1972) *Camberwell Reception Centre*, Institute of Psychiatry.

United Nations Social Defence Research Institute (1976) *Economic Crises and Crime*, Rome: UNSDRI.

Vold, G. B. (1958) *Theoretical Criminology* (Ch. 9, Economic Conditions and Criminality), Oxford University Press.

Vinson, T. and Homel, R. (1965) 'Crime and disadvantage', *British Journal of Criminology*, 15 (1): 21–31.

Walker, N. (1987) *Crime and Criminology: A Critical Introduction*, Oxford University Press.

Walton, D. (1987) 'The residential, employment and educational needs of offenders' in, Harding, J. (ed), *Probation and the Community: A Practice and Policy Reader*, London: Tavistock.

West, J. and Martin, P. (1979) 'Employment and unemployment in the English inner cities', *Department of Employment Gazette*, August: 746–9, 752.

West, D. J. (1982) *Delinquency: Its Roots, Careers and Prospects*, London: Heinemann.

—— and Farrington, D. P. (1977) *The Delinquent Way of Life*, London: Heinemann.

Wilkins, L. T. (1963) 'What is crime?' *New Society*, (2) 15–16.

Winchester, S. and Jackson, H. (1982) 'Residential burglary', Home Office Research Study no. 74, London: HMSO.

Winter, J. M. (1982) 'Economic instability and infant mortality in England and Wales, 1920–1950', in, J. M. Winter (ed.), *The Working Class in Modern British History*, Cambridge University Press.

Yeager, M. G. (1979) 'Unemployment and imprisonment', *Journal of Criminal Law and Criminology*, 70: 586–8.

Index